COMPUTER
MODELS OF THE
SHOE, LEATHER, HIDE SEQUENCE

1959 Award Winner

THE FORD FOUNDATION DOCTORAL DISSERTATION SERIES

A dissertation submitted in partial fulfillment of the requirements for the degree of Doctor of Philosophy at Carnegie Institute of Technology

COMPUTER

MODELS OF THE

SHOE, LEATHER, HIDE SEQUENCE

KALMAN J. COHEN

Graduate School of Industrial
Administration, Carnegie
Institute of Technology

1960

PRENTICE - HALL , INC .

Englewood Cliffs, N. J.

Foreword

This volume is one of five doctoral dissertations selected for publication in the first annual Doctoral Dissertation Competition sponsored by the Program in Economic Development and Administration of The Ford Foundation. The winning dissertations were completed during the academic year 1958-59 by doctoral candidates in business administration and doctoral candidates in the social sciences and other fields relevant to the study of problems of business.

The dissertation competition is intended to generalize standards of excellence in research on business by graduate students. It should give widespread professional recognition to persons recently awarded doctorates in business whose dissertation research is especially distinguished by its analytical content and strong roots in the underlying disciplines. It is also intended to give recognition to a select number of persons outside business schools who in their doctoral dissertations pursued with distinction interests relevant to business.

The dissertations selected include, in addition to Dr. Cohen's monograph:

Budget Control and Cost Behavior
    Andrew C. Stedry
    Graduate School of Industrial Administration
    Carnegie Institute of Technology

The Structure of a Retail Market and the Market Behavior of Retail Units
    Bob R. Holdren
    Department of Economics
    Yale University

Polya Type Distributions in Renewal Theory, with an Application to an Inventory Problem
    Frank Proschan
    Department of Statistics
    Stanford University

Some Personality Determinants of the Effects of Participation
    Victor H. Vroom
    Department of Psychology
    University of Michigan

v

The many high-quality dissertations submitted were judged by the most exacting professional standards. Specific criteria included:

a. Importance of the problem and originality of approach;
b. Use of the most appropriate and powerful tools of analysis;
c. Clear relation to the relevant theoretical framework or a contribution to theory;
d. Direct relevance to the practice of business or management;
e. Clarity and effectiveness of presentation.

An examination of all five volumes in this series will reveal that four of the five make considerable use of mathematical and statistical tools. This reflects the increasing importance of modern quantitative methods in the study of business. On the other hand, the use of quantitative techniques should certainly not be considered a *sine qua non* of rigorous research in business. It is hoped that in future years it will be possible to select for publication a greater number of nonmathematical dissertations of the highest quality.

On behalf of The Ford Foundation, I wish to express my sincere appreciation to the Editorial Committee for its painstaking effort in selecting the winning dissertations. The scholars who served as members of the Committee for the first year's competition were Robert Ferber, Research Professor of Economics, University of Illinois; Sherman J. Maisel, Professor of Business Administration, University of California (Berkeley); and William Foote Whyte, Professor, New York State School of Industrial and Labor Relations, Cornell University.

The work of the Editorial Committee was materially aided by a group of six readers, who spent hundreds of hours in conscientious examination of the dissertations submitted. The Foundation and the Committee wish to thank Professors Austin C. Hoggatt and Julius Margolis of the University of California (Berkeley), Henry A. Landsberger and Seymour Smidt of Cornell University, and Vernon K. Zimmerman and Thomas A. Yancey of the University of Illinois for their service as readers in the first year of the competition.

Finally, my colleagues and I wish to acknowledge the substantial contribution of Prentice-Hall, Inc., to the publication and distribution of the selected dissertations.

THOMAS H. CARROLL
VICE PRESIDENT
THE FORD FOUNDATION

New York, New York
January, 1960

Preface

This thesis discusses the construction of two mathematical models describing the aggregate behavior of shoe retailers, shoe manufacturers, and cattlehide leather tanners between 1930 and 1940. The BLS consumers' price index, disposable personal income, and the stocks of hides held by hide dealers are the chief exogenous variables. The major endogenous variables are the retailers' selling price, sales, and shoe receipts; the manufacturers' selling price, production, and leather receipts; the tanners' selling price, finished production, hide wettings, and hide receipts; and the hide dealers' selling price.

The mathematical form of the models is a complex, nonlinear system of lagged simultaneous difference equations subject to boundary constraints, with one month as the basic time period. The models are designed for simulation rather than analytical solution; hence, an electronic digital computer is used to trace out the time paths from 1930 to 1940 of each endogenous variable. One of the models, a "one-period-change model," is intended to explain the values of the endogenous variables for only one time period ahead into the future; this model assumes, as is usually done in econometrics, that lagged endogenous variables refer to their actually observed values. Our other model, a "process model," is designed to explain the determination of the endogenous variables for an arbitrarily large number of future time periods. The equations of the process model, together with the observed time paths of the exogenous variables, are treated as a closed dynamic system; each month, the values of the predetermined endogenous variables are the values generated by the model, not the actually observed values. The methodology of this "closed dynamic system" approach, i.e., of process models, is compared with the methodology underlying the one-period-change models which are traditional in econometrics, with particular attention being paid to the problems of parameter estimation and of validation (i.e., "goodness of fit") of the models.

The time paths of the major endogenous variables which are traced out by both models are compared with the observed time paths of these

Preface

variables from 1930 through 1940. The results indicate that comparisons on an annual basis show a very close correspondence between the time paths generated by our process model and the actual values. Although our models do not provide a completely acceptable monthly aggregate level description of the shoe, leather, hide sequence between 1930 and 1940, the evidence provided by the annual comparisons is consistent with the hypothesis that the models incorporate some of the mechanisms which determined the behavior of individual firms in these industries (although no precise statistical tests have been made).

ACKNOWLEDGEMENTS

To my Thesis Committee at the Graduate School of Industrial Administration, Carnegie Institute of Technology, under whose direction this paper was completed, I extend my deepest appreciation. By the constant encouragement and the competent criticisms of Professors Richard M. Cyert, Merton H. Miller, and Franco Modigliani, Chairman, the quality of this research has been considerably improved. In addition to his role as a member of the Thesis Committee, Professor Cyert has greatly aided this work in his function as Director of the Behavioral Theory of the Firm Project, under whose program this report has been prepared. The research has been supported by grants of the Graduate School of Industrial Administration from the School's research funds and from funds provided by the Ford Foundation for the study of organizational behavior.

This work could not have been undertaken without the generous cooperation of Mrs. Ruth P. Mack. In addition to the wealth of empirical information and theoretical insights contained in her book, *Consumption and Business Fluctuations*, Mrs. Mack has provided me with considerable amounts of data from her private files at the National Bureau of Economic Research and with some extremely kind words of encouragement throughout this project.

In thanking Mrs. Mack and Professors Cyert, Miller, and Modigliani for the help that they have extended, I want to make clear that any defects which remain in the product are the sole responsibility of the author.

Special acknowledgements must be extended to the staff of the Computation Center at the Carnegie Institute of Technology for making available so freely all of their facilities. Much of the programming was done using the Internal Translator, a scientific compiler developed at Carnegie by Professor Alan J. Perlis, Mr. Joseph W. Smith, and Mr.

Harold R. Van Zoeren. Special disk routines written by Mr. Alex Federowicz and Mr. Van Zoeren were also used. I would especially like to thank Mr. Arthur Evans, Jr. for modifying to my own specifications an automatic time series plotting program he originally wrote for the Jones and Laughlin Steel Corporation.

My greatest debt in this project is to my wife, Joan, whose encouragement, versatility, and help have made this work possible in more ways than I can ever count.

KALMAN J. COHEN

Contents

COMPUTER
MODELS OF THE
SHOE, LEATHER, HIDE SEQUENCE

CHAPTER 1

Introduction

"Economics is the study of how the goods and services we want get produced, and how they are distributed among us.... Economists look at the economic system in two ways. One way is to look at its behavior in the aggregate.... This approach they call 'macro-economics'.... The other way is to look at the individual businesses and people who underlie the aggregates of macro-economics.... This approach economists call 'micro-economics'. ...You don't have to take a course in economics to see that these two approaches are all intertwined."[1]

Economists, in their teaching and research, all too frequently forget these interconnections. The goal of micro-economic theories is generally the analysis of price determination and the effects of prices on the allocation of specific resources to particular uses. The goals of macro-economic theories, in contrast, are usually the determination of the levels of national income and aggregate resource employment.

Prices are not completely absent from macro theories, and income concepts do play a role in micro theories. However, the determination of individual incomes is simply part of the general

---

[1]George Leland Bach, *Economics: An Introduction to Analysis and Policy*, Englewood Cliffs, N. J.: Prentice-Hall, Inc., 2nd ed., 1957, pp. 3-4.

pricing processes for micro theories. While prices are relevant to macro theories, "macro theorists usually abstract from the problems of determining individual prices and their relations to one another and deal with aggregate price indices as determined by the level of aggregate spending. Since the problems of individual price determination are assumed away in macro theory, the relationship between the individual units and the aggregates is not clear."[1]

The need to clarify the relations between the behavior of individual units and the aggregates they comprise became very apparent to Mrs. Ruth P. Mack when she attempted "to answer the [important macro-economic] question: What part does consumer buying play in business cycles?"[2] Mrs. Mack found that a satisfactory answer could not be obtained without a better understanding of the ways in which business firms react to changes in purchases by consumers than that provided by the neoclassical theory of the firm. In seeking to obtain sufficiently detailed information about the behavior of individual firms, Mrs. Mack was led to undertake her study of the shoe, leather, hide sequence. "In attacking the problem posed, I have chosen the method of a case study of a single industry. There were several reasons for the choice. Primarily, it was predicated on the paucity or poor quality of broad series of monthly data.... The second difficulty with the aggregate approach derives from the fact that even a quick exploration showed that *it would be necessary to study the detailed purposes and techniques of businessmen,* as well as the history of sales and output. *This excursion into how businessmen understand, formulate, and conquer their problems seemed essential to learning which are the purposeful and which the passive sectors of change,* and, consequently how the telling questions about processes must be phrased.... As the work progressed, a positive

---

[1] James M. Henderson and Richard E. Quandt, *Microeconomic Theory*, New York: McGraw-Hill Book Co., 1958, pp. 2-3.

[2] Ruth P. Mack, *Consumption and Business Fluctuations: A Case Study of the Shoe, Leather, Hide Sequence*, New York: National Bureau of Economic Research, 1956, p. 9.

reason for the case study became evident: *the method is especially well suited to analysis of the dynamic interconnection between adjacent stages.*[1]

In recent years, the development of high speed computers and of a methodology for computer simulation of economic models[2] has progressed to the point where computer models[3] can be constructed to help us understand the detailed aspects of business behavior and the dynamic interactions among firms which Mrs. Mack feels are necessary before we can explain the role of "consumer buying in business cycles." One of the great deficiencies still existing in macro-economic models is the weakness which comes from inadequate micro theory. In attempting to understand such macro phenomena as economic growth and business

---

[1]*Ibid.* Italics added.

[2]See, for example:

(a) R. M. Cyert, E. A. Feigenbaum, and J. G. March, "Models in a Behavioral Theory of the Firm," Behavioral Theory of the Firm Project Working Paper No. 8, Graduate School of Industrial Administration, Carnegie Institute of Technology, December, 1957. Presented to The Econometric Society, December 29, 1957, Philadelphia, Pennsylvania. Also published in *Behavioral Science*, Vol. 4, No. 2 (April, 1959), pp. 81-95.

(b) James S. Dusenberry, Otto Eckstein, and Gary Fromm, "A Simulation of the United States Economy in Recession," presented to The Econometric Society, December 28, 1958, Chicago, Illinois.

(c) Jay W. Forrester, "Industrial Dynamics — A Major Breakthrough for Decision Makers," *Harvard Business Review*, Vol. 36, No. 4, July – August, 1958, pp. 37-66.

(d) Austin C. Hoggatt, "Simulation of the Firm," Research Paper RC-16, IBM Research Center, Poughkeepsie, New York, August 15, 1957.

(e) Austin C. Hoggatt and Frederick E. Balderston, "Models for Simulation of an Intermediate Market," presented to The Econometric Society, December 29, 1958, Chicago, Illinois.

(f) Guy H. Orcutt, Martin Greenberger, and Alice M. Rivlin, "Decision-Unit Models and Simulation of the United States Economy," (mimeographed), Harvard University, January, 1958.

(g) Joseph V. Yance, "Simulation of a Model of Production and Prices," presented to The Econometric Society, August 26, 1958, Cambridge, Massachusetts.

[3]In this thesis, we use the term "computer model" to denote a special kind of formal mathematical model, namely, a model which is not intended to be solved analytically but rather to be simulated on an electronic digital computer. Simulating a computer model consists in programming a digital computer to trace out numerically the time paths generated by the model for all of its endogenous variables.

cycles, economists of necessity have had to assume simplified decision rules for firms and consumers. Some of these simplifications were required by the methodology followed in macroeconomics, but most of them stemmed directly from our ignorance of the processes whereby behavior is determined at the level of individual firms and individual households.

The greatest advantage of computer models lies in their ability to provide precise quantitative predictions while still encompassing the richness and complexity of the world. In order to use simulation methodology most effectively, considerably more effort must be devoted to collecting empirical information concerning individual firms' decision rules than has hitherto been done.

If computer models are successfully used for studying microeconomic behavior, then it is no longer necessary that entrepreneurial decision-making be explainable in terms of a single "general" theory of the firm. Numerous "special" theories can be used, provided only that we can catalogue the sectors of the world in terms of the proper special theories. Models of the type developed in this thesis for simulating the behavior of individual firms have broad implications for macro-economics, micro-economics, and management science.

This thesis is designed to explore ways in which electronic digital computers can be used as a tool of economic investigation and to increase our understanding of the dynamics of the shoe, leather, and hide industries. The major respect in which this dissertation differs from previous simulation work in economics is the extent to which an attempt is made to simulate the behavior of a specific portion of the economy in a particular time period. Our intention is ultimately to understand entrepreneurial decision-making in the shoe, leather, hide sequence and to demonstrate this understanding by reproducing segments of the behavior of firms in these industries between 1930 and 1940.

The problems connected with the formulation of an economic model for digital simulation, the computer realization of the model, and the testing of the model are sufficiently great to make it premature to attempt within the scope of a doctoral dissertation a simulation of the entire national economy. To gain an awareness of these problems and find methods for overcoming them, we decided to construct some computer models of the shoe, leather, hide sequence. There were two reasons for choosing to work with these industries. First, they form a relatively manageable vertically related segment of the economy with little horizontal leakage: most cattle hides are tanned into leather, most cattlehide leather is made into shoes, and most shoes are sold at retail. Second, a considerable body of empirical knowledge has been gathered about these industries, thanks largely to the painstaking work of Mrs. Mack.[1]

To realize the full potential of using computer simulation techniques in the study of the shoe, leather, hide sequence, it would be desirable to have micro-economic models specifying the mechanisms governing the behavior of individual firms. This development remains on the agenda for future research. The models discussed in this paper, Models II and II E,[2] deal only with aggregate sectors. Even at this level, numerous methodological problems arose in the attempted simulations, problems which still remain to be solved.

Since one of our reasons in formulating models of the shoe, leather, hide sequence is to explore the usefulness of computer models in economics, we would like to structure these models so that they shed as much light as possible upon the benefits which might be obtained from wider use of simulation techniques. We feel that the greatest advantages of computer models will be obtained from models which are formulated at a micro-economic

---

[1]*Op. cit.* Mrs. Mack has generously allowed me to use data from her private files at the National Bureau of Economic Research.

[2]Model I, our first formulation of the shoe, leather, hide model, contained so many defects that it no longer seems worth discussing. It was described in Kalman Joseph Cohen, "A Computer Model of the Shoe, Leather, Hide Sequence," Behavioral Theory of the Firm Project Working Paper No. 11, Preliminary Version, Graduate School of Industrial Administration, Carnegie Institute of Technology, December, 1958, presented at a joint session of The Econometric Society and the American Statistical Association, Chicago, Illinois, December 27, 1958.

level. Such models can go into great detail concerning the determinants of the behavior of individual firms and individual households, and they may ultimately enable us to answer classes of questions which seem to elude more traditional economic theories.[1]

In order to gain some experience with the kinds of problems arising in simulation models which describe the detailed processes governing the behavior of individual firms, insofar as it is feasible our models are formulated in terms of behavioral mechanisms pertaining to individual firms. In effect, we investigate the extent to which aggregate behavior in the shoe, leather, hide sequence can be explained by the "typical firm" approach, i.e., by assuming that an economic sector as a whole behaves in the same manner as would a representative firm belonging to that sector.

In formulating our models of the shoe, leather, hide sequence we have tried to conform as closely as possible to the hypotheses about the behavior of firms in these industries that were spelled out in Mrs. Mack's book. Many of these relations were stated only in qualitative terms. A computer simulation model requires that all of its relations be stated in explicit quantitative form. Therefore, it has been necessary to add to Mrs. Mack's hypotheses numerous specific assumptions which are not contained in her book. For this and other reasons, we do not intend that any of these models should be viewed as a test of the analysis contained in that book. There are a myriad of ways in which a literary exposition of a body of economic theory can be translated into a formal mathematical model, and the failure of any formal model to explain adequately the behavior of its endogenous variables cannot be interpreted necessarily as a defect of the underlying literary exposition.

---

[1]A few examples of the kinds of questions we have in mind are:
  (a) What are the processes by which selling prices are determined in an oligopolistic firm?
  (b) What are the processes by which the allocation of resources within a firm are determined?
  (c) What are the effects of changing the internal communication structure on the production and pricing decisions of a firm?

Two models of the shoe, leather, hide sequence are formulated in Chapter 3. They differ only in that Model IIE is a "one-period-change model," i.e., is intended to explain the values of the endogenous variables for only one period ahead into the future; whereas Model II is a "process model" i.e., is designed to explain the determination of the endogenous variables for an indefinitely large number of future time periods. The distinction between process models and one-period-change models is amplified in Chapter 2. After a description in Chapter 4 of how the models were simulated on a computer, Chapter 5 compares the time paths of the major endogenous variables traced out by both models with the observed values of these variables from 1930 through 1940. In Chapter 6, the implications of our results concerning the relations between individual firms and aggregate behavior and the relations between process models and one-period-change models are discussed, and directions for future work in this area are outlined.[1]

---

[1]Dr. Joseph V. Yance has independently developed another simulation of the shoe leather, hide sequence ("Simulation of a Model of Production and Prices," *op. cit.*) Dr. Yance's model is more closely related to the general models describing retail wholesale, factory systems developed by Professor Jay Forrester ("Industrial Dynamics — A Major Breakthrough for Decision Makers," *op. cit.*) than it is to the model which is implicit in Mrs. Mack's work. The general results of these "Industrial Dynamics" models show that a simultaneous system of difference or differential equations with arbitrary time lags and adjustment coefficients can produce oscillatory time paths, the timing and amplitude of the fluctuations depending essentially on the nature of these time lags and adjustment coefficients. Instead of fitting his model by using actual data, Dr. Yance adjusts the parameters until they produce time paths in accord with his a priori notions of reasonableness.

CHAPTER 2

Process Models in Dynamic Economics

Before turning to a detailed description of the shoe, leather, hide models, we must consider the characteristics of the world that we are attempting to explain. Any economic model is, to a greater or lesser extent, a description of the world. To date, the least ambiguous descriptions of the economic world have generally been provided by that sub-class of economic models known as "econometric models."

In an econometric model, "we view the economic system as describable by a set of simultaneous equations expressing all the interrelationships among the measurable economic magnitudes which guide economic behavior. The variables in this set of equations are classified into two main types, endogenous and exogenous. The endogenous variables are those variables which are determined within the system of economic forces in a narrow sense.... The exogenous variables are those which represent forces outside the confines of the economic system."[1]

---

[1]Lawrence R. Klein, *Economic Fluctuations in the United States, 1921-1941*, Cowles Commission for Research in Economics, Monograph No. 11, New York: John Wiley and Sons, Inc., 1950, p. 2.

An economic model is a special construct by means of which a body of economic theory can be translated into specific descriptions of the world. "Economists have, over a period of years, developed theories of economic behavior which are the basis for the determination of our endogenous variables.... Entrepreneurs, households, speculators are assumed to behave according to some fundamental rational patterns, which can often be written in the form of mathematical equations.... [These equations] are called structural equations because they show the basic structure of the economic system.... Our system is complete when the number of equations in the entire set of structural equations is just enough to determine all the endogenous variables, given the exogenous variables. We must develop as many structural equations as we have endogenous variables. For the 'explanation' of exogenous variables we do not attempt to develop any structural equations."[1]

A completely specified econometric model contains only particular equations in which all the parameters have been given numerical values. Such models are the most concrete forms in which economists have tried to describe the world. Each structural equation states the manner in which one endogenous variable is determined by the values of other endogenous variables, exogenous variables, and (usually) one or more random terms.

To see clearly what is asserted about the world by an econometric model, consider a simple model presented by Klein for expository purposes.[2] The following notation is used:

$C(t)$ = consumption in year t;
$W_1(t)$ = private wage bill in year t;
$W_2(t)$ = government wage bill in year t;
$\pi(t)$ = non-wage income (profits) in year t;
$I(t)$ = net investment in year t;
$K(t)$ = stock of capital at the end of year t;
$Y(t)$ = output in year t;

[1] *Ibid.*, pp. 3-4.
[2] *Ibid.*, pp. 58-80.

$T(t)$ = business taxes in year t;

$G(t)$ = government and net foreign demand in year t.

All of these variables are expressed in real terms, i.e., in constant dollars.

Klein's model consists of only six equations; the series $W_2(t)$, $\pi(t)$, and $G(t)$ are exogenous variables. The model can be written as follows:[1]

(I)
$$
\begin{cases}
C(t) = \alpha_0 + \alpha_1 [W_1(t) + W_2(t)] + \alpha_2 \pi(t) + u_1(t) \\
I(t) = \beta_0 + \beta_1 \pi(t) + \beta_2 \pi(t-1) + \beta_3 K(t-1) + u_2(t) \\
W_1(t) = \gamma_0 + \gamma_1 [Y(t) + T(t) - W_2(t)] + \gamma_2 [Y(t-1) \\
\qquad\qquad + T(t-1) - W_2(t-1)] + \gamma_3(t) + u_3(t) \\
K(t) = K(t-1) + I(t) \\
Y(t) = W_1(t) + W_2(t) + G(t) \\
T(t) = C(t) + I(t) + G(t) - Y(t)
\end{cases}
$$

In these equations, the α_i, β_i, and γ_i are parameters to be replaced by numerical values, and the $u_i(t)$ are random variables with some specified joint distribution function.

Twenty years ago, most econometricians interested in estimating the values of the parameters in the first three equations in (I) would have applied least squares regression analysis to each equation separately. One of the major advances in econometric methodology within the past two decades has been the discovery that applying least squares procedures directly to the structural equations produces numerical estimates of the parameters which are biased and inefficient, because the assumptions of the Markov least squares theorem are not generally satisfied by the structural equations.[2] Superior estimates of the parameters in a model can usually be made by procedures which explicitly take into account the simultaneous character of the relations incorporated in the model.

---

[1]*Ibid.*, pp. 65-66.

[2]See, for example, Lawrence R. Klein, *A Textbook of Econometrics*, Evanston, Illinois: Row Peterson and Co., 1953, Chap. III.

The nature of the joint determination which is hypothesized by the econometric model can be seen more clearly if it is recast into the following form:

(II)
$$
\begin{cases}
C(t) = \alpha_0 + \alpha_1 [W_1(t) + \overline{W_2(t)}] + \alpha_2 \overline{\pi(t)} \\
I(t) = \beta_0 + \beta_1 \overline{\pi(t)} + \beta_2 \overline{\pi(t-1)} + \beta_3 \overline{K(t-1)} \\
W_1(t) = \gamma_0 + \gamma_1 [Y(t) + T(t) - \overline{W_2(t)}] + \gamma_2 \overline{[Yt - 1)]} \\
\qquad + \overline{T(t-1)} - \overline{W_2(t-1)}] + \gamma_3 t \\
K(t) = \overline{K(t-1)} + I(t) \\
Y(t) = W_1(t) + \overline{W_2(t)} + \overline{G(t)} \\
T(t) = C(t) + I(t) + \overline{G(t)} - Y(t)
\end{cases}
$$

In writing the equations of (II), a bar has been placed above every predetermined (exogenous and lagged endogenous) variable. The resulting simultaneous system of six independent equations is sufficient to determine the values (strictly speaking, the *expected* values, since the random error terms have been dropped) of the six current endogenous variables: $G(t)$, $I(t)$, $W_1(t)$, $K(t)$, $Y(t)$, and $T(t)$. Equations (II) are assumed to hold for $t = 1, 2, 3, \cdots$.

The way in which Klein's simple model is intended as a description of the world is shown clearly by (II). The model states that for any year t, the values of $C(t)$, $I(t)$, $W_1(t)$, $K(t)$, $Y(t)$, and $T(t)$ can be determined by the simultaneous solution of the system which results when the barred predetermined variables are replaced by their known values. This is an empirical assertion about the nature of the world which, in principle, is capable of verification or refutation.

Assuming that the structure of the model does not change between year t and year $t + 1$, the model states a similar fact about the values of $C(t + 1)$, $I(t + 1)$, $W_1(t + 1)$, $K(t + 1)$, $Y(t + 1)$, and $T(t + 1)$, a fact which may be derived simply by replacing t with $t + 1$ in (II). In this statement about the world in year $t + 1$, it is important to note that the predetermined endogenous variables which are assumed to be known are endogenous variables referring to year t, not to year $t - 1$.

The assertions made by the Klein model about the nature of the world are, in a very strict sense, assertions only about the behavior of the world for one year, and only one year, into the future. Given the *known* values of the lagged endogenous variables in year $t - 1$ and of the exogenous variables in both years t and $t + 1$, the equations in (II) state something very definite about the nature of the world in year t, but they say nothing about the nature of the world in year $t + 1$. An *ad hoc* attempt at forecasting the values of $C(t + 1)$, $I(t + 1)$, $W_1(t + 1)$, $K(t + 1)$, $Y(t + 1)$, and $T(t + 1)$ based only on the information stated in the preceding sentence could be made by inserting this information in equations (II) to obtain forecasts of $K(t)$, $Y(t)$, and $T(t)$. These forecasted values could then be used in place of the known values in the system which results when t is replaced by $t + 1$ in (II). Strictly speaking, however, the econometric model is not intended to be used in this manner. The techniques for estimating the values of parameters which, according to accepted theory, should be used with econometric models are not intended to yield good results in multi-period forecasts.[1]

In essence, traditional econometric models are intended to describe only changes from one period to the next period. They are not evolutionary models which attempt to describe the complete unfolding of a dynamic process over time. Most econometric models have been estimated and tested in such a way that they can be considered to be *one-period-change* models.[2] As such, they can serve to only a limited degree as translations into concrete terms of what most dynamic economic theories intend to assert about the world.

---

[1]"A more difficult problem is encountered in forecasting several periods ahead in which lagged values [of the endogenous variables] needed to predict . . . [the future endogenous variables in which we are interested] have not yet occurred and need to be forecasted. In this situation we pile error upon error, and predictions in advance become cumulatively less reliable as we go farther and farther into the future." *Ibid.*, pp. 252-253.

[2]A possible noteworthy exception is Colin Clark, "A System of Equations Explaining the United States Trade Cycles, 1921 to 1941," *Econometrica*, Vol. 17 (1949), pp. 93-124.

When an electronic digital computer is used to simulate an economic theory, the theory is usually formulated in terms of a system of lagged simultaneous difference equations. The computer then traces out the time paths of each endogenous variable. The equations of the model, together with the observed time paths of the exogenous variables, are treated as a closed dynamic system; each period, the values of the predetermined endogenous variables are the values generated by the model, not the known or actually observed values. The methodology of the closed dynamic system approach, i.e., of *process models*, differs from the methodology underlying more traditional econometric models mainly in the treatment of lagged endogenous variables. In the one-period-change model, it is assumed that each period any errors resulting from the "determination" of last period's endogenous variables are corrected, so that there is a tendency for the one-period-change model to be kept on course by the fact that it always has a correct starting place. The process model, on the other hand, is forced to live with any errors that may have been made by the model, in "determining" the values of the endogenous variables in previous periods; there is no automatic resetting of the error terms to assure a correct jumping off place for each period.

Equations (II) are the formulation of the simple Klein model as a one-period-change model. If the Klein model were intended to be a process model, it would have to be formulated as shown on page 14:

$$(\text{III}) \begin{cases}
C(1) = \alpha_0 + \alpha_1 [W_1(1) + \overline{W_2(1)}] + \alpha_2 \overline{\pi(1)} \\
I(1) = \beta_0 + \beta_1 \overline{\pi(1)} + \beta_2 \overline{\pi(0)} + \beta_3 \overline{K(0)} \\
W_1(1) = \gamma_0 + \gamma_1 [Y(1) + T(1) - \overline{W_2(1)}] \\
\qquad\quad + \gamma_2 \overline{[Y(0) + T(0)]} - \overline{W_2(0)} + \gamma_3 \\
K(1) = \overline{K(0)} + I(1) \\
Y(1) = W_1(1) + \overline{W_2(1)} + \overline{G(1)} \\
T(1) = C(1) + I(1) + \overline{G(1)} - Y(1) \\
C(2) = \alpha_0 + \alpha_1 [W_1(2) + \overline{W_2(2)}] + \alpha_2 \overline{\pi(2)} \\
I(2) = \beta_0 + \beta_1 \overline{\pi(2)} + \beta_2 \overline{\pi(1)} + \beta_3 K(1) \\
W_1(2) = \gamma_0 + \gamma_1 [Y(2) + T(2) - \overline{W_2(2)}] \\
\qquad\quad + \gamma_2 [Y(1) + T(1) - W_2(1)] + 2\gamma_3 \\
K(2) = K(1) + I(2) \\
Y(2) = W_1(2) + \overline{W_2(2)} + \overline{G(2)} \\
T(2) = C(2) + I(2) + \overline{G(2)} - Y(2) \\
C(3) = \alpha_0 + \alpha_1 [W_1(3) + \overline{W_2(3)}] + \alpha_2 \overline{\pi(3)} \\
I(3) = \beta_0 + \beta_1 \overline{\pi(3)} + \beta_2 \overline{\pi(2)} + \beta_3 K(2) \\
W_1(3) = \gamma_0 + \gamma_1 [Y(3) + T(3) - \overline{W_2(3)}] \\
\qquad\quad + \gamma_2 [Y(2) + T(2) - \overline{W_2(2)}] + 3\gamma_3 \\
K(3) = K(2) + I(3) \\
Y(3) = W_1(3) + \overline{W_2(3)} + \overline{G(3)} \\
T(3) = C(3) + I(3) + \overline{G(3)} - Y(3) \\
\qquad\qquad \vdots
\end{cases}$$

In equations (III), a bar above a variable is again used to denote a predetermined variable. Comparing equations (II) and (III) brings out clearly the differences between one-period-change models and process models. The particular one-period-change model is a simultaneous system of six independent equations determining six endogenous variables. The particular process model, in contrast, is a simultaneous system of $6N$ independent equations determining $6N$ endogenous variables, where N is potentially infinite. Furthermore, several predetermined variables in the one-period-change model, namely $K(t-1)$, $Y(t-1)$, and $T(t-1)$ for $t \geq 2$, are simultaneously[1] determined variables in the process model.

To obtain estimates of the structural parameters in a process model which are unbiased and efficient, the simultaneous nature of the relations incorporated in the model must be considered explicitly. In principle, this leads to very large systems of simultaneous equations. The nature of this task is several orders of magnitude more difficult for process models than it is for one-period-change models.

Whereas most traditional econometric models can make assertions about the world concerning only one-period changes, process models can make statements about N-period changes in the world, for any positive integer N. Hence, process models are intended to say a great deal more about the nature of the world than are most econometric models. Any economic theory, therefore, has a much higher likelihood of *incorrectly* describing the world when formulated as a computer model than when formulated as a one-period-change model.

All the previous attempts at applying computer simulation techniques to study economic phenomena with which we are familiar have treated the equations of the model and the observed time paths of the exogenous variables as closed dynamic systems,

---

[1]In this context, "simultaneously" is used in its mathematical rather than its temporal sense.

i.e., they have all been formulated as process models.[1] It should be quite clear, however, that this is not the only way in which digital computers can be useful in exploring the consequences of a model. There is no reason why a computer cannot be used to trace out the one-period changes which are determined by a traditional econometric model. If the structural equations in an econometric model are either very numerous or highly nonlinear, an electronic computer may be the most practical tool for determining the values of the current endogenous variables which the model yields.

In the following section two models of the shoe, leather, hide sequence are described. One of these, Model II, is a process model. To the equations of Model II, the required past history, i.e., the actual values of some of the variables prior to 1930, and the observed time paths of the exogenous variables between 1930 and 1940 are adjoined. The resulting system is then used to generate time paths for all the endogenous variables between 1930 and 1940.[2] Our other model, Model IIE, is a one-period-change model, in which lagged values of the endogenous variables are replaced by their actually observed values. If our models were completely and correctly to describe the world, the time paths so generated would exactly coincide with the observed time paths of the endogenous variables. To the extent that they do not, our models fail to be an adequate description of the world.

----

[1]The distinction between what traditional econometric models seem to assert about the nature of the world and what "traditional" (if this term may be applied to so young a field) computer simulation models seem to assert about the nature of the world is so sharp that we once used the term "econometric model" for what we now call "one-period-change model" and the term "computer model" for what we now call "process model." See Kalman Joseph Cohen, "A Computer Model of the Shoe, Leather, Hide Sequence," Behavioral Theory of the Firm Project Working Paper No. 11, Preliminary Version, Graduate School of Industrial Administration, Carnegie Institute of Technology, December, 1958, presented at a joint session of The Econometric Society and the American Statistical Association, Chicago, Illinois, December 27, 1958.

[2]Although Mrs. Mack's study of the shoe, leather, hide sequence generally applied to the entire interwar period, 1930 is the earliest year for which the *complete* set of required data was readily obtainable

CHAPTER 3

General Description of the Shoe, Leather, Hide Models

3.1. Overall Structure of Model II

The shoe, leather, and hide industries form a tightly connected vertical sequence of economic sectors in which there is relatively little horizontal leakage. Most cattle hides enter into commerce as direct or indirect by-products of the meat packing industry. These cattle hides are sold by the packers and other hide dealers to tanners, who convert the hides into cattlehide leather. The bulk of this leather is sold to shoe manufacturers for fabrication into shoes, and most shoes in the United States are made from cattlehide leather. The shoes flow through various distribution channels into the hands of shoe retailers, who in turn sell them to the public.

The shoe, leather, hide sequence can be divided into five important vertical segments: consumers, shoe retailers, shoe manufacturers, cattlehide leather tanners, and hide dealers (including meat packers).[1] The major economic variables of these

---

[1]Shoe wholesalers might be inserted as a separate segment between retailers and manufacturers. However, this would be only a partial layer, since some retailers buy shoes directly from some manufacturers. To deal with wholesalers in our models would require considerably more information about separate transactions between retailers, wholesalers, and manufacturers. Hence, we shall ignore the separate existence of wholesalers, in effect including the purchases and inventories of wholesalers with those of retailers in what might be called a "distributors' segment." We shall simply use the label "retailers' segment."

groups on which attention is focused are the consumers' purchases of shoes; the selling prices of retailers, manufacturers, tanners, and hide dealers; and the purchases and production of retailers, manufacturers, and tanners. We are interested in constructing a formal model which will explain the determination of the monthly values of these economic variables from 1930 through 1940. Since the shoe, leather, and hide industries form a tightly connected vertical sequence, the major exogenous variables which need be included are disposable personal income and the BLS consumers' price index (which affect the top of the sequence through their impact on consumers' behavior) and hide stocks in the hands of hide dealers (which affect the bottom of the sequence through their impact on hide dealers' behavior.)[1]

The quantitative information available for estimating and testing our models pertains only at the aggregate sector level; that is, we have data on the selling prices, production, and purchases of all retailers as a group, all manufacturers as a group, all tanners as a group, etc. While trying to obtain models which explain the aggregate behavior of retailers, manufacturers, and tanners, we would also like to explore the implications of some of the hypotheses suggested by Mrs. Mack concerning the behavior of individual firms in the retailing and manufacturing segments. Chapter 1 mentioned that one objective of this thesis was to explore some ways in which digital computers and computer simulation techniques can contribute to economic theory. Our basic working principle was that the greatest benefits from computer models can ultimately be obtained from models formulated at a micro-economic level: models which attempt to describe the detailed processes governing the behavior of individual firms and individual households. Wherever feasible, the shoe, leather, hide models will be formulated in terms of behavioral

---

[1]Average seasonal indices for some of the endogenous variables between 1930 and 1940 are introduced into a few of the regression equations in our models as exogenous terms, which means that we make no attempt to explain the seasonal pattern for some of the variables.

mechanisms describing the actions of individual firms. In effect, we shall try to determine the degree to which the aggregate behavior of shoe retailers and shoe manufacturers (the only sectors for which Mrs. Mack presents sufficiently detailed information to make this possible) can be explained by the "typical firm" approach, i.e., by supposing that retailers as a group behaved in the same way that a typical retailer would and that manufacturers as a group behaved in the same way that a typical manufacturer would. For the consumers', tanners', and hide dealers' segments, because of the nature of the hypotheses set forth by Mrs. Mack, there is no alternative other than adopting directly an aggregate sector level of "explanation."

Before presenting the detailed relations which comprise our models of the shoe, leather, hide sequence, a brief survey will be provided. Our models are formulated in terms of two major classes of variables, prices and physical flows. The major prices which are endogenously determined are retail shoe price, factory shoe price, leather price, and hide price. The major physical flows which are determined by the models are retailers' sales and receipts of shoes; manufacturers' production of shoes and receipts of leather; and tanners' finished leather production, hide wettings, and hide receipts.

In our models, the dollar expenditures on shoes by consumers are determined entirely by exogenous variables: disposable personal income and a seasonal factor.[1] The physical volume of retailers' sales is simply the consumers' expenditures divided by the retail price of shoes. The retailers' receipts of shoes are determined basically by demand considerations accompanied by some price speculation on inventories: retailers always try to have available for sale at least enough shoes to meet their anticipated demand; the extent to which they try to push their inventory levels beyond this point depends upon their changing evaluations of future market prospects. The manufacturers plan their shoe

---

[1]Provided that retailers' have available for sale at least the required number of pairs of shoes.

production in response to retailers' orders for shoes, spreading these orders evenly over the available lead time to obtain some smoothing of production. The leather purchases by manufacturers are designed at least to provide for their current production requirements, but the manufacturers frequently build up their leather inventories beyond current needs in response to price speculation motives. The production of finished leather by tanners depends upon the relation between their leather shipments and their leather stocks, but, because tanners attempt to smooth production rates, finished leather production is also tied to the previous month's production and hide wettings. Tanners' hide wettings depend upon the turnover rate of tanners' finished leather stocks, but again efforts are made to prevent rapid changes from occurring in the rate of production. Tanners' purchases of hides are determined by a reduced form relation reflecting both their current needs (the higher the rate of wettings, the more hides the tanners will order) and their view of the supply situation (the lower the price of hides last month, the more hides tanners will buy).

The retail price of shoes is determined in our models by a rigid markup on factory shoe prices. In setting the factory shoe price, manufacturers consider both the strength of consumer demand and the costs of production, as reflected in recent leather prices. Current leather price depends upon lagged leather price and current and lagged hide prices. Current hide price is determined in our model as a reduced form which reflects interactions between supply and demand considerations. The supply aspects are summarized in the final reduced form equation in terms of the ratio of leather and hide stocks in the hands of buyers to the leather and hide stocks in the hands of sellers; the higher this ratio, the lower the relative size of sellers' inventories, and the higher the price the sellers require to induce them to sell hides. The demand side is reflected in the reduced form equation by actual uses of hides by tanners, i.e., by hide wettings and finished leather production, and by factory shoe price, which serves as a proxy for underlying forces causing shifts in the demand schedule for hides.

There are several important interactions between prices and physical flows in our models. The physical volume of retail shoe sales is directly affected by retail shoe price. Retailers' purchases of shoes, manufacturers' purchases of leather, and tanners' purchases of hides are affected, largely through price speculation on inventories, by prices which are endogenously determined in Model II. The most important converse effect in our models is the dependence of hide price upon the purchases of leather by manufacturers and the finished leather production, hide wettings, and hide purchases by tanners.

Following a glossary of the symbols used in our models, the detailed relations which comprise Model II are presented in Sections 3.3 through 3.7.

3.2. Glossary of Symbols

$Bls(t)$ — BLS consumers' price index in month t, 1935–39 = 100.

$Dpi(t)$ — Disposable personal income in month t, \$.

$Fp(t)$ — Factory shoe price (manufacturers' selling price of shoes) in month t, \$/pair.

$Fp^*(t)$ — Average cost to retailers (on an average valuation basis) of shoes available for sale at retail in month t, \$/pair.

$G(t)$ — Manufacturers' leather stocks at end of month t, equivalent hides.

$G^s(t)$ — Manufacturers' finished shoe stocks at end of month t, pairs.

$H(t)$ — Retailers' shoe stocks at end of month t, pairs.

$h^*(t)$ — Retailers' "minimum desired" number of shoes available for sale at retail in month t, pairs.

$Hp(t)$ — Average price of hides in month t, \$/equivalent hide.

$Hp^I(t)$ Imported hides price in month t, \$/pound.

$Hp^P(t)$ Packer hides price in month t, \$/pound.

$Hp^R(t)$ Hide price ratio in month t: the ratio of the average of country hides price and imported hides price to packer hides price, all in month t, pure number.

$J^H(t)$ Tanners' stocks of hides at end of month t, equivalent hides.

$J^I(t)$ Tanners' stocks of in-process leather at end of month t, equivalent hides.

$J^L(t)$ Tanners' stocks of finished leather at end of month t, equivalent hides.

$L(t)$ Manufacturers' leather receipts in month t, equivalent hides.

$Lp(t)$ Leather price in month t, \$/equivalent hide.

$Lp_{min}(t)$ Lowest leather price during the last six months, \$/equivalent hide.

$M_{Hp^R}(t)$ Average seasonal index in month t for hide price ratio from 1930 through 1940, per cent.

$M_Q(t)$ Average seasonal index in month t for tanners' orders for all hides from 1930 through 1940, per cent.

$M_{R^D}(t)$ Average seasonal index in month t for tanners' receipts of domestic hides from 1930 through 1940, per cent.

$M_{R^P}(t)$ Average seasonal index in month t for tanners' receipts of packer hides from 1930 through 1940, per cent.

$M_{[SRp]}(t)$ Average seasonal index in month t for retail dollar shoe sales from 1930 through 1940, per cent.

$M_W(t)$ Average seasonal index in month t for tanners' hide wettings from 1930 through 1940, per cent.

$M_X(t)$ Average seasonal index in month t for tanners' finished leather production from 1930 through 1940, per cent.

$P(t)$ Shoe production in month t, pairs.

$Q(t)$ Tanners' orders for all hides in month t, equivalent hides.

$Q^c(t)$ Tanners' orders for country hides in month t, equivalent hides.

$Q^I(t)$ Tanners' orders for imported hides in month t, equivalent hides.

$Q^P(t)$ Tanners' orders for packer hides in month t, equivalent hides.

$R(t)$ Tanners' receipts of all hides in month t, equivalent hides.

$R^c(t)$ Tanners' receipts of country hides in month t, equivalent hides.

$R^D(t)$ Tanners' receipts of domestic hides in month t, equivalent hides.

$R^I(t)$ Tanners' receipts of imported hides in month t, equivalent hides.

$R^P(t)$ Tanners' receipts of packer hides in month t, equivalent hides.

$Rp(t)$ Retail price of shoes in month t, \$/pair.

$S(t)$ Retailers' shoe sales in month t, pairs.

$[SRp]\,(t)$ Retailers' shoe sales in month t, \$.

$W(t)$ Tanners' hide wettings (hides entering the leather production process) in month t, equivalent hides.

$X(t)$ Finished leather production in month t, equivalent hides.

$\Gamma(t)$ Hide stocks in the hands of packers, butchers, and hide dealers at the end of month t, equivalent hides.

μ Abbreviational variable used in the determination of retailers' shoe orders.

ν Abbreviational variable used in the determination of retailers' shoe orders.

ρ Abbreviational variable used in the determination of manufacturers' leather purchases.

ρ^* Abbreviational variable used in the determination of manufacturers' leather purchases.

$\Sigma(t)$ Retailers' receipts of shoes in month t, pairs.

$\Omega^\theta(t)$ Retailers' shoe orders placed in month t for delivery in month $t + \theta$, pairs.

In order to distinguish between *ex ante* and *ex post* values of the same time series variable, a time subscript is used to denote a value anticipated or planned for the variable; the date of the subscript indicates (the end of) the month when the anticipation was held or the plan made. Thus, $S_{t-1}(t + \tau)$ denotes the anticipation held by retailers at the end of month $t - 1$ (which is the same as the start of month t) of retail shoe sales in month $t + \tau$.

PARAMETERS

α A weighting parameter in the retailers' sales anticipations rules.

$C_{i,j}$ The ith coefficient in the linear regression equation number j. (The constant term in the jth regression equation is $C_{0,j}$.)

$C_h{}^*$ Retailers' "minimum desired" shoe stock for a zero rate of sales, pairs.

m_l Manufacturers' lower "acceptable" margin over leather costs per pair of shoes, \$/pair.

m_u Manufacturers' upper "acceptable" margin over leather costs per pair of shoes, \$/pair.

r_l Institutionally acceptable "long limit" on turnover ratio of manufacturers' leather stocks, per month.

r_s Institutionally acceptable "short limit" on turnover ratio of manufacturers' leather stocks, per month.

Rpmu   Ratio of retailers' margin over cost price to retail selling price, i.e., the "percentage" markup on retail shoe prices.

λ Amount of leather required to manufacture one pair of shoes, equivalent hides/pair.

3.3. Consumers' Expenditures on Shoes

The major role of consumers in the shoe, leather, hide sequence is buying shoes from retailers. Although other interactions exist,[1] shoe purchases are the only aspect of consumer behavior that is explained in our models.

Mrs. Mack has found[2] that consumers' dollar expenditures on shoes can be adequately described as a linear function of consumers' income, relative shoe prices (i.e., retail shoe price divided by the BLS consumers' price index), and a time trend to account for changing tastes. Using seasonally adjusted monthly data for all of the variables and fitting a least squares regression equation for 1929-1941, Mrs. Mack found that the equation

$$(1) \qquad [SRp](t) = C_{0,1} + C_{1,1}Dpi(t) + C_{2,1}\frac{Rp(t)}{Bls(t)} + C_{3,1}t$$

has a multiple correlation coefficient of .98 and regression

---

[1]The household sector receives a portion of its income from wages, salaries, rent, interest, and profits paid out by firms in the shoe, leather, and hide industries; the labor costs and production functions of firms in these industries are affected by particular aspects of household behavior. Since the shoe, leather, hide sequence is only a small sector of the overall economic activity in the United States, the main causal chains connecting consumers with firms in the shoe, leather, hide sequence is unidirectional. In our models, therefore, we shall suppose that consumers' incomes and tastes are exogenous factors, but that consumers' purchases of shoes are endogenously determined.

[2]Mack, *op. cit.*, pp. 65-68.

coefficients which are all statistically significant at the 5 per cent level or better.[1]

This result cannot be directly incorporated into our models which are formulated in terms of monthly data uncorrected for seasonal adjustments. Consumers' shoe purchases exhibit a strong seasonal pattern which is definitely not present in disposable personal income and relative shoe prices. Hence, equation (1) could not be expected to perform very well if seasonally unadjusted monthly data were used.[2] The easiest procedure for introducing the proper seasonality in equation (1) would be to add an exogenous variable whose value each month is the average seasonal index for that month for 1930-1940. In replacing equation (1) by the following equation

$$(2) \quad [SRp](t) = C_{0,2} + C_{1,2}Dpi(t)$$
$$+ C_{2,2}\frac{Rp(t)}{Bls(t)} + C_{3,2}t + C_{4,2}M_{[SRp]}(t)$$

neither $C_{2,2}$ nor $C_{3,2}$ were statistically significant at the 5 per cent level.[3,4] Dropping the relative shoe price and the time trend terms

---

[1]Mrs. Mack's findings are consistent with a much earlier study by von Szeliski and Paradiso. Using annual data for 1919 and 1921-1933, the latter found that consumers' per capita expenditures on shoes were explained by shoe prices, national income, and a time trend. Von Szeliski and Paradiso also found that dollar expenditures by consumers for shoes are much more stable than the number of pairs purchased. "It appears that the consumers tended to set aside a certain fraction of the national income for the purchase of shoes, depending on the price of shoes, and that considerable doubt exists only as to the *way* in which this fixed or determined fund is spent, whether for a few pairs of shoes at a high price, or more pairs of shoes at a low price." (p. 341) See Victor S. von Szeliski and L. J. Paradiso, "Demand for Boots and Shoes as Affected by Price Levels and National Income," *Econometrica*, Vol. 4 (1936), pp. 338-355.

[2]Using seasonally unadjusted data for 1930-1940 in equation (1) produces a multiple correlation coefficient adjusted for degrees of freedom of only .55.

[3]In fitting all of the regression equations used in Model II, no variable was retained unless there was a probability of at least 95 per cent that the coefficient of that variable was non-zero. According to Hald, *Statistical Theory with Engineering Applications*, p. 639, to test the hypothesis that an estimated regression coefficient has a true value of zero, a two-tailed t test is applied to the ratio of the estimated regression coefficient to its standard error, using $n-m-1$ degrees of freedom, where n is the number of observations and m is the number of independent variables. With 120 degrees of freedom (a slightly low number for all of our regression equations,

from equation (2) resulted in a satisfactory explanation for consumers' expenditures on shoes:

(3) $[SRp](t) = C_{0,3} + C_{1,3}Dpi(t) + C_{2,3}M_{[SRp]}(t)$

All the regression coefficients in equation (3) are statistically significant at the 5 per cent level or better. The estimates of these coefficients and (in parentheses) the number of times each estimate exceeds its standard error are:

$C_{0,3} = -69,800,000$

$C_{1,3} = .0147$ (19.2)

$C_{2,3} = 910,000$ (37.9)

The multiple correlation coefficient adjusted for degrees of freedom is .97. Equation (3) is used in Model II as the determinant of consumers' expenditures on shoes.[1]

3.4. Retailers' Behavior

The major economic variables at the retailers' sector are the selling price, sales, and receipts of shoes. We want to describe realistically the processes governing the behavior of a typical retailer, and then examine the extent to which these behavioral mechanisms could account for the observed behavior of all retailers as a group. At the retail level, Mrs. Mack has provided a wealth of information out of which it is possible to fabricate a structural framework for the behavior of our mythical typical retailer along all of the dimensions in which we are interested.

---

which were always fitted to 132 monthly observations), a regression coefficient must exceed its standard error by at least 1.98 in order to be statistically significant at the 5 per cent level.

[4]The estimates of the coefficients of (2) and (in parentheses) the number of times each estimate exceeds its standard error are:

$C_{0,2} = -105,000,000$	$C_{3,2} = -37,400$ (1.1)
$C_{1,2} = .0149$ (12.2)	$C_{4,2} = 914,000$ (40.1)
$C_{2,2} = 1,240,000,000$ (1.6)	

The multiple correlation coefficient adjusted for degrees of freedom is .97.

[1]This equation implies that the demand for shoes is unit elastic with respect to shoe price.

At the retail level, selling price behavior is fairly straight-forward. Mrs. Mack states[1] that retailers' pricing is generally a constant percentage markup over cost price. For 1927-39, this markup averaged 41 per cent over factory price. Both for convenience and to smooth fluctuations in factory price, we use an *average cost* valuation method for determining retail price. Thus, the retailers' pricing behavior is given by

$$(4) \qquad Rp(t) - Fp^*(t) = Rpmu \, Rp(t)$$

or

$$(5) \qquad Rp(t) = \frac{Fp^*(t)}{1 - Rpmu}$$

where

$$(6) \quad Fp^*(t) = [H(t-1)Fp^*(t-1) + \Omega^0(t) \, Fp(t)$$
$$+ \, \Omega^1(t-1) \, Fp(t-1) + \Omega^2(t-2) \, Fp(t-2)$$
$$+ \, \Omega^3(t-3) \, Fp(t-3)] \div [\Sigma(t) + H(t-1)]$$

Following Mrs. Mack, in Model II we shall take $Rpmu = .41$.

Given the consumers' expenditures on shoes determined by equation (3), the number of pairs of shoes sold by retailers is simply the consumers' expenditures divided by the average retail selling price of shoes (provided that at least this number of pairs of shoes are available for sale by being either in the initial inventory of retailers or arriving in shipments that month). Hence,

$$(7) \qquad S(t) = \min\left[\frac{[SRp](t)}{Rp(t)}, H(t-1) + \Sigma(t) \right]$$

The sales anticipations of retailers, i.e., the forecasts made by retailers concerning their own future sales, are important intervening variables in Model II. The receipts of shoes by retailers are determined by the orders for shoes which are placed by retailers, and these shoe orders in turn are partially dependent upon the retailers' forecasts of their own future sales. For the most part, shoes are ordered by retailers to meet their anticipated future sales requirements.

---

[1]*Op. cit.*, pp. 46, 104-105.

One of the mechanisms presented by Mrs. Mack[1] to account for the sales anticipations of retailers is:

(8) $S_{t-1}(t + \tau) =$

$$S(t + \tau - 12) \frac{S(t - 1) + S(t - 2) + S(t - 3)}{S(t - 13) + S(t - 14) + S(t - 15)}$$
$$\text{for } \tau = 0, 1, \cdots, 11$$

When equation (8) was used as the sales forecasting rule in an earlier version of the shoe, leather, hide model undesirably large fluctuations in retailers' orders for shoes were produced by a coupling of the amplification and extrapolation of past sales trends incorporated in equation (8) with the retailers' ordering rules. As a result of this experience, we decided to dampen some of these extreme fluctuations by adopting for Model II the following less explosive form of sales forecasting rules:

(9) $S_{t-1}(t + \tau) =$

$$\alpha\, S(t + \tau - 12) \frac{S(t - 1) + S(t - 2) + S(t - 3)}{S(t - 13) + S(t - 14) + S(t - 15)}$$
$$+ (1 - \alpha)S(t + \tau - 12), \qquad \text{for } \tau = 0, 1, \cdots, 11$$

In effect, equation (9) takes as the retailers' sales forecasts a weighted average of the forecasts given by the mechanism suggested by Mrs. Mack and the sales of the corresponding month a year ago.[2] The manner in which the numerical value of the weighting parameter α was determined will be discussed below.

There are various delivery terms under which retailers can purchase shoes from manufacturers. It is both realistic and convenient to suppose that four basic types of orders may be placed by retailers at the beginning of a month: orders for immediate delivery (within the current month), for delivery one

---

[1] *Ibid.*, pp. 105-110.

[2] A very similar rule was used by Robert Ferber to explain the forecasts of car loadings made by railroad shippers, the principal difference being that our equation (9) is formulated in terms of monthly data whereas Ferber's rule dealt solely with quarterly data. See Robert Ferber, *The Railroad Shippers' Forecasts*, Studies in Business Expectations and Planning, Urbana, Illinois: The University of Illinois, 1953, esp. Chap. IV.

month hence, for delivery two months hence, and for delivery three months hence.

"When the new lines are first assembled and shown by shoe manufacturers, usually in November and December or early January for Easter styles, and in May or June for the fall models, retailers place 'preseason' advance orders which may cover between 35 and 65 per cent of estimated sales for the next six months.[1] ... As the season progresses, 'secondary' orders are placed for delivery in perhaps two months, more or less.[2] In addition, retailers typically order some goods for 'at-once' delivery; and in this case the receipt of the order may be expected within a few weeks or even less, sometimes in a few days if the shoe is carried by the 'in-stock' department of a manufacturer or wholesaler, or it may not be expected for six weeks or so if it must be made to order and factories are active.[3] These orders for immediate delivery may take care of unexpected developments or they may simply be quite routine fill-in orders, or they may represent the slack in the 'open-to-buy' position intentionally left to 'sweeten stocks' at the latest possible moment. . . .

"The basic picture, then, is of a battery of orders that converge to supply the desired receipts of a given month. Desired receipts, in turn, consist of merchandise expected to be sold plus the intended increase (or minus the decrease) in stocks. Of course, both desired receipts and desired stock change may shift as the future unfolds."[4]

In Model II all orders are delivered as expected. Hence:

$$(10) \quad \Sigma(t) = \Omega^0(t) + \Omega^1(t-1) + \Omega^2(t-2) + \Omega^3(t-3)$$

and

$$(11) \quad H(t) = H(t-1) + \Sigma(t) - S(t)$$

In determining the size of the orders that they place, one of

---

[1] These are the $\Omega^3(t)$ orders in Model II.
[2] These are the $\Omega^2(t)$ orders in Model II.
[3] These are the $\Omega^0(t)$ and the $\Omega^1(t)$ orders in Model II.
[4] Mack, *op. cit.*, pp. 99-100.

the key variables closely considered by retailers is the level of their inventories, both actual and desired. Mrs. Mack suggests[1] that the retailers' "desired" inventory level at the start of any month is determined by:

(12) $h^*(t) = h^*(t - 1) + k[S(t) - S(t - 1)]$

The graph of equation (12) is shown in Figure 1.

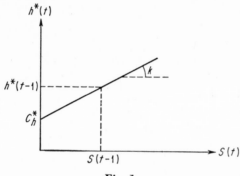

Fig. 1

Mrs. Mack concludes[2] that under stable market conditions, retailers intend to keep an incremental stock-sales ratio of *one*, i.e., that $k = 1$ in equation (12), i.e.,

(13) $h^*(t) = h^*(t - 1) + S(t) - S(t - 1)$

which implies:

(14) $h^*(t) = C_{h*} + S(t)$

The manner in which the numerical value of the parameter C_{h*} was determined is discussed below.

Equation (14) indicates the "minimum desired" inventory level which retailers would like to have if they were actually to know what their sales would be in the current month. At the start of the month, however, retailers must base their desires on anticipated rather than actual sales. Thus, retailers always want to have at least

---

[1]*Ibid.*, p. 99.
[2]*Ibid.*, p. 112.

(15) $$h^*_{t-1}(t) = S_{t-1}(t) + C_{h*}$$

pairs of shoes available for sale during the current month. If this level is not provided by inventory on hand plus shipments scheduled for arrival this month, retailers will place an order for immediate delivery to make up the deficit. The following equation describes the immediate delivery ordering behavior of retailers:

(16) $$\Omega^0(t) = h^*_{t-1} - [H(t-1) + \Omega^1(t-1) + \Omega^2(t-2) + \Omega^3(t-3)],$$

subject to $\Omega^0(t) \geq 0$

Orders for immediate delivery are more costly and offer a poorer selection of shoes than orders for longer term delivery. Retailers do not plan to use immediate delivery orders at some future date in preference to longer term delivery orders based on anticipated future requirements. Therefore, retailers try to obtain their shoe requirements for the $(t+1)$st month by placing in month t an order for delivery in one month. The retailers' "minimum desired" number of shoes available for sale in month $t+1$ as foreseen at the start of month t is:

(17) $$h^*_{t-1}(t+1) = S_{t-1}(t+1) + C_{h*}$$

Letting

(18) $$H_{t-1}(t) = H(t-1) + \Omega^0(t) + \Omega^1(t-1) + \Omega^2(t-2) + \Omega^3(t-3) - S_{t-1}(t)$$

then the mechanism determining retailers' orders for delivery one month hence can be stated:

(19) $$\Omega^1(t) = h^*_{t-1}(t+1) - [H_{t-1}(t) + \Omega^2(t-1) + \Omega^3(t-2)],$$

subject to $\Omega^1(t) \geq 0$

There are two definite and distinct selling seasons for retail shoes. Based on the monthly sales index numbers that Mrs. Mack gives,[1] the retail selling seasons can be divided into March through August (spring and summer) and September through February

---

[1] *Ibid.*, p. 98 and p.142n.

(autumn and winter). Within each season, the same shoes ("spring–summer" or "autumn–winter") are considered sold.

In Model II, primary orders are placed at the beginning of December for the spring–summer season and at the beginning of June for the fall–winter season; secondary orders are placed at the beginning of March for the spring–summer season and at the beginning of September for the fall–winter season. Hence,

(20) $\Omega^2(t) = 0$ for $t =$ Jan., Feb., Apr., May, June, July, Aug., Oct., Nov., Dec.

(21) $\Omega^3(t) = 0$ for $t =$ Jan., Feb., Mar., Apr., May, July, Aug., Sept., Oct., Nov.

The behavioral mechanism that is adopted in Model II for retailers' secondary shoe orders assumes that the purpose of these orders is to provide for any still uncovered portions of the entire season's sales requirements, as foreseen at the start of the season when the order is placed. Thus:

(22) $H_{t-1}(t+1) = H_{t-1}(t) + \Omega^1(t) + \Omega^2(t-1) + \Omega^3(t-2)$
$- S_{t-1}(t+1)$

(23) $h^*_{t-1}(t+2) = S_{t-1}(t+2) + C_{h^*}$

and

(24) $\qquad \Omega^2(t) = h^*_{t-1}(t+2) - [H_{t-1}(t+1) + \Omega^3(t-1)]$
$+ \sum_{\tau=3}^{5} S_{t-1}(t+\tau) \qquad\qquad$ for $t =$ Mar., Sept.

subject to $\Omega^2(t) \geq 0$

The fraction of anticipated sales of the season which are still uncovered when secondary orders are placed depends upon the size of the primary or preseason order. This, in turn, depends upon the retailers' evaluation of market prospects, for more preseason orders are placed when times are good than when times are bad.

"Several different sorts of factors could contribute to the resultant tendency for orders having relatively long delivery terms to form a larger proportion of all orders in good times than in bad. In good times, the bargaining position of sellers is strong relative to that of buyers, and sellers prefer early orders which permit more economical factory operation. In good times, buyers anticipate slower deliveries for three reasons: it takes longer for orders to be put into production; a longer time is required to complete production; stocks of finished shoes from which immediate deliveries can be made are relatively small."[1]

Mrs. Mack also states[2] that in more prosperous times, retailers place a larger proportion of preseason orders because they expect the wholesale prices of shoes to rise over the selling season, so they tend to speculate on prices. In practice, however, retailers expect wholesale prices to rise in those periods when delivery is expected to be tight, and vice versa. It is sufficient to consider a single composite retailers' expectation concerning shifting market prospects.

The retailers' behavioral mechanism determining preseason orders is given by:

$$(25) \quad \Omega^3(t) = h^*_{t-1}(t + 3) - H_{t-1}(t + 2) - S_{t-1}(t + 3)$$
$$+ \mu \sum_{\tau=3}^{8} S_{t-1}(t + \tau) \qquad \text{for } t = \text{June, Dec.}$$

$$\text{subject to } \Omega^3(t) \geq 0$$

In equation (25), μ is the fraction of the season's sales requirements ordered at the start of month t on a preseason, three-month delivery basis. This depends on the retailers' views about "market prospects," which are interpreted in the following manner:

$$(26) \qquad\qquad \mu = \tfrac{1}{3}(1 - \nu) + \nu$$

$$\text{subject to } \mu \leq 1$$

where

$$(27) \quad \nu = \frac{Hp(t - 1) - Hp(t - 4)}{Hp(t - 4)} \qquad \text{if } Hp(t - 1) \geq Hp(t - 4)$$

$$\nu = 0 \text{ otherwise}$$

Equations (26) and (27) are consistent with Mrs. Mack's observations. She says[3] that in hand-to-mouth buying, 30 or 35

---

[1] *Ibid.*, p. 121.
[2] *Ibid.*
[3] *Ibid.*, p. 116.

per cent of expected sales for next season are bought when the new
lines are first shown. ($\mu \geq 33.3$ per cent is well within the minimum range.) In a sellers' market, this proportion might be 60, 65,
100 per cent or even more.

$$\mu = 60 \text{ per cent if } \nu = 40 \text{ per cent}$$

$$\mu = 65 \text{ per cent if } \nu = 47.5 \text{ per cent}$$

$$\mu = 100 \text{ per cent if } \nu = 100 \text{ per cent})$$

In measuring retailers' views of changing market prospects, we
adopt one of Mrs. Mack's suggestions[1] and use the most recent
three-month change in hide prices.

The following two equations define the remaining terms of
equation (25):

(28) $H_{t-1}(t+2) = H_{t-1}(t+1) + \Omega^3(t-1) - S_{t-1}(t+2)$

and

(29) $h_{t-1}^*(t+3) = S_{t-1}(t+3) + C_{h*}$

The behavioral mechanisms of retailers incorporated in Model
II contain two parameters, α and C_{h*}, whose numerical values
have not yet been determined. Both of these parameters play
an essential role in the rules describing retailers' orders for shoes.
If actual data on retailers' orders from 1930-1940 were available,
this information could be used to estimate the numerical values
of α and C_{h*} which yield the closest fit between our model and
the observed orders series. This approach is closed, however,
because the actual orders data are unavailable for that time
period. The method actually followed utilized retailers' shoe
stocks as a surrogate for the missing orders series.

The numerical values of α and C_{h*} were estimated to provide
the closest overall fit between the inventory series generated by
our model and the observed inventories. Equations (9) through
(29) of the retailers' segment were treated as a separate subsystem,
with *ex post* sales, $S(t)$, and average hide prices, $Hp(t)$, as exog-

---

[1]*Ibid.*, p. 142.

enous variables. To this subsystem of equations, the observed values of both $S(t)$ and $Hp(t)$ from 1930-1940 and the appropriate amount of past history for each variable prior to 1930 were adjoined, resulting in a closed dynamic system which could generate values of retailers' inventories, orders, and receipts.[1] The exact time paths traced by these variables depended upon the numerical values assigned to the two parameters α and C_{h*}.

This subsystem was simulated using a large number of values for both α and C_{h*} until that pair of parameter values was found which minimized the sum of $[\hat{H}(t) - H(t)]^2$ from January, 1930 through December, 1940,[2] where $\hat{H}(t)$ is the time path for retailers' shoe inventories generated by the subsystem and $H(t)$ is the observed time path. By this criterion, the best values for these parameters were:

$$\alpha = .001$$
$$C_{h*} = 170,000,000$$

These were the values used in Model II.[3]

3.5. Manufacturers' Behavior

Factory selling price, shoe production, and leather receipts are the major economic variables at the manufacturers' level. We would like to obtain the behavioral mechanisms which describe the actions of a typical manufacturer and to determine the extent that these mechanisms explain the actual behavior of manufacturers as a group. Although the information which Mrs. Mack

---

[1]This subsystem was simulated as a process model, i.e., lagged values of the variables endogenous to this subsystem were taken to be those values generated previously by the subsystem.

[2]Since α and C_{h*} are nonlinear parameters in this subsystem, and since retailers' shoe stocks is not a continuous function of these parameters, *ad hoc* numerical methods were used to find the parameter values which minimized the criterion function. The most successful method consisted in casting successively finer grids or meshes over the parameter space, centering the exploration on those areas of the parameter space which seemed to contain relative minimum points of the criterion function.

[3]The very low value resulting for α means that equation (9) determining retailers' sales anticipations is a highly regressive forecasting rule.

has given about the manufacturing sector is not as detailed as her discussion of retailers' behavior, enough material is provided from which to construct a behavioral framework for most of the actions of our mythical typical manufacturer.

Manufacturers' purchases of leather are received in the same month that they are placed.[1] The following inventory identities result:

(30) $G(t) = G(t - 1) + L(t) - \lambda P(t)$

(31) $G^s(t) = G^s(t - 1) + P(t) - \Omega^0(t) - \Omega^1(t - 1) - \Omega^2(t - 2) - \Omega^3(t - 3)$

Mrs. Mack clearly states that the production of shoes by manufacturers is closely tied to the retailers' orders for shoes. "The specialty of the product is too great to permit extensive manufacture of anything except the particular style, color, material, size, and width of shoe that someone has ordered. Shoe manufacturers testify to this, claiming that most shoes in this country are made to order.... The notion of a tight link between sales and production seems to be supported by scraps of statistical data.... The conclusion emerges that production in shoe factories is undertaken primarily in direct or indirect response to specific orders, though, of course, there is a penumbra of seasonal anticipation of demand, or of work undertaken on the basis of advices less binding to the customer than a confirmed order."[2]

In Model II, manufacturers produce only those shoes that retailers order. To help smooth production rates, manufacturers spread the production over the entire lead period available for

---

[1]"Shoe manufacturers purchase leather in a market in which suppliers (primarily tanners) carry large stocks of finished leather . . . . Small lots of leather can often be obtained within a day or so, plus time in transit. When markets are weak, very substantial lots may be obtained in the same way . . . . The speed with which leather can be obtained is testified to by the fact that a thirty-day supply seems commonly to be considered adequate for the efficient mechanical operation of a shoe factory. This means that a substantial proportion of leather can actually be on hand in time to meet production schedules if it is purchased somewhere between two to six weeks ahead of the day when work on the shoe orders is scheduled to start." Mack, *op. cit.*, pp. 142-143.

[2]*Ibid.*, p. 142.

filling the orders, with some production taking place during the month of delivery. The manufacturers' production behavior is determined by the following rule:

$$(32)\ P(t) = \tfrac{1}{4}[\Omega^3(t - 3) + \Omega^3(t - 2) + \Omega^3(t - 1) + \Omega^3(t)]$$
$$+ \tfrac{1}{3}[\Omega^2(t - 2) + \Omega^2(t - 1) + \Omega^2(t)]$$
$$+ \tfrac{1}{2}[\Omega^1(t - 1) + \Omega^1(t)] + \Omega^0(t)$$

The shoe manufacturers' selling prices are relatively inflexible. Other than this observation, Mrs. Mack's only clear hypothesis about manufacturers' selling price is that it is geared to expectations regarding consumer behavior. What price changes are made seem to be of a cyclical, rather than a subcyclical nature.[1]

It should be possible to tie manufacturers' pricing policies to the BLS price index and disposable personal income, for these are variables which Mrs. Mack found influenced consumers' expenditures on shoes. Because the bargaining between manufacturers and retailers over factory shoe prices definitely considers the perceived effect of prices on consumers' expenditures, these variables are important. Another variable which might be introduced is the largest component of manufacturing costs, namely current or recent leather costs.

Lacking any additional hypotheses by Mrs. Mack concerning the determination of factory selling price, no obvious way suggests itself for defining a behavioral mechanism explaining the setting of manufacturers' selling price for shoes. The only recourse is to seek a regression equation determining factory price as a function of those variables which our theory suggests are important. Instead of behavioral mechanisms, we fall back upon the level of "explanation" which is traditional in aggregate econometric work.

The following regression equation was considered for the determination of factory shoe price:

---

[1] *Ibid.*, pp. 149-151.

(33) $Fp(t) = C_{0,33} + C_{1,33}Bls(t-1) + C_{2,33}Dpi(t-1)$
$+ C_{3,33}[Lp(t-1) + Lp(t-2) + Lp(t-3)$
$+ Lp(t-4) + Lp(t-5) + Lp(t-6)] \div 6$

All of the regression coefficients in equation (33) are statistically significant at the 5 per cent level or better. The single equation least squares estimates of these coefficients and (in parentheses) the number of times each estimate exceeds its standard error are:

$C_{0,33} = -.972$

$C_{1,33} = .0244 \ (20.5)$

$C_{2,33} = -.769 \times 10^{-10} \ (7.8)$

$C_{3,33} = .0749 \ (7.7)$

The multiple correlation coefficient adjusted for degrees of freedom is .97. Since equation (33) seems highly satisfactory, it is incorporated into Model II as the determining function for factory shoe price.

The manufacturers' leather purchases must be sufficient to meet production requirements, but frequently manufacturers take a long position in leather going far beyond their current production needs. The reasons for manufacturers changing their ownership positions in leather relate to speculating on price, insuring delivery, and obtaining better selections.[1] In expanding or contracting their leather inventories in accordance with shifting market prospects, the manufacturers are constrained by institutionally imposed limits called the "long-short market range."[2] These can be stated in terms of the turnover rate of manufacturers' leather stocks:

(34) $$r_l \geq \frac{\lambda P(t)}{G(t)} \geq r_s$$

Substituting equation (30) in (34) results in:

(35) $$r_l \geq \frac{\lambda P(t)}{G(t-1) + L(t) - \lambda P(t)} \geq r_s$$

---

[1] *Ibid.*, pp. 145-146.
[2] *Ibid.*, pp. 160-162.

Solving (35) for $L(t)$:

(36) $$\frac{\lambda P(t)}{r_s} \geq G(t - 1) + L(t) - \lambda P(t) \geq \frac{\lambda P(t)}{r_l}$$

and

(37) $$\lambda P(t)\left(1 + \frac{1}{r_s}\right) - G(t - 1) \geq L(t)$$
$$\geq \lambda P(t)\left(1 + \frac{1}{r_l}\right) - G(t - 1)$$

The long-short market range restricts $L(t)$ between the upper and lower limits given in (37). Two additional constraints have precedence over (37), however. These are that leather shipments be nonnegative, i.e., that

(38) $$L(t) \geq 0$$

and that manufacturers order at least enough leather to satisfy their current production requirements, i.e., that

(39) $$L(t) \geq \lambda P(t) - G(t - 1)$$

Hence, subject to the constraints imposed by (38) and (39), a weighted average of the upper and lower limits given in (37) is the behavioral mechanism determining manufacturers' receipts of leather. That is, manufacturers' leather purchases are explained by the equation:

(40) $$L(t) = (1 - \rho)\left[\left(1 + \frac{1}{r_l}\right)\lambda P(t) - G(t - 1)\right]$$
$$+ \rho\left[\left(1 + \frac{1}{r_s}\right)\lambda P(t) - G(t - 1)\right]$$

subject to the constraints (38) and (39). In equation (40),

$$0 \leq \rho \leq 1$$

How is ρ determined? Mrs. Mack suggests[1] that the primary influence on ρ stems from the tolerable limits on margins:

(41)   if $Fp(t - 1) - \lambda Lp(t - 1) \leq m_l$, then $\rho = 0$

        if $Fp(t - 1) - \lambda Lp(t - 1) \geq m_u$, then $\rho = 1$

---

[1]*Ibid.*, pp. 162-165.

In order for manufacturers to want to extend their position in leather, it is necessary for their production to be increasing. "It is not likely that prices will be expected to rise unless sales are rising, or to fall unless sales are falling. Appropriate behavior of sales thus becomes a necessary though not a sufficient condition to changes in market-prospect-tied buying."[1] To measure "changes in sales" conditions, $P(t) - P(t - 12)$ is used. Unless leather prices are expected to rise, there is no reason for manufacturers to extend their leather stocks beyond the institutionally permitted short position. Hence,

(42) $\quad \rho = 0$ if $m_l < Fp(t - 1) - \lambda Lp(t - 1) < m_u$ and

$\qquad$ if $P(t) < P(t - 12)$

Mrs. Mack says[2] that extension of the manufacturers' ownership position depends upon their expectation of increasing leather prices (represented by recent increases in hide prices) and the certainty with which this expectation is held (represented by the level of leather prices). A simple representation of this mechanism would be the following. Let

(43) $\quad Lp_{\min}(t) = \min [Lp(t - 1), Lp(t - 2), \cdots, Lp(t - 6)]$

i.e., $Lp_{\min}(t)$ is the lowest leather price in the last half year. Let ρ^* be a simple average of the past quarter's percentage change in hide prices and the percentage by which last month's leather price exceeds the lowest leather price in the past half year, i.e.,

(44) $\quad \rho^* = \left(\dfrac{1}{2}\right)\dfrac{Hp(t - 1) - Hp(t - 4)}{Hp(t - 4)}$

$\qquad + \left(\dfrac{1}{2}\right)\dfrac{Lp(t - 1) - Lp_{\min}(t)}{Lp_{\min}(t)}$

Then:

(45) $\quad$ if $m_l < Fp(t - 1) - \lambda Lp(t - 1) < m_u$ and
$\qquad$ if $P(t) > P(t - 12)$, then:

---

[1] *Ibid.*, p. 146.
[2] *Ibid.*, pp. 155-162.

$$\rho = \rho^* \quad \text{if } 0 \le \rho^* \le 1$$
$$\rho = 0 \quad \text{if } \rho^* < 0$$
$$\rho = 1 \quad \text{if } \rho > 1$$

The numerical values of five parameters, λ, r_s, r_l, m_l, and m_u, contained in the behavioral mechanisms of manufacturers developed for Model II remain to be specified. Values for these parameters were found in the following way.

The average amount of leather required to produce one pair of shoes can be found by dividing the domestic consumption of cattlehide leather by the shoe production for domestic consumption, since our models assume that cattlehide leather is used only for shoes,[1] and the production and sales figures employed exclude rubber shoes.[2] Using actual monthly data for 1930–1940 and averaging the monthly ratios of domestic consumption of cattlehide leather to shoe production for domestic consumption results in a value of $\lambda = .0505$ equivalent hides per pair.

The criterion for choosing the numerical values of r_s, r_l, m_l, and m_u was to obtain the closest overall fit between the leather receipts series generated by Model II and the observed manufacturers' receipts of leather. Equations (38) through (45) of the manufacturers' segment were treated as a separate process submodel. To this subsystem, the observed values of $Hp(t)$, $Lp(t)$, $P(t)$, $G(t)$, and $Fp(t)$ and the appropriate amount of past history were adjoined, resulting in a complete process model

---

[1]"While cattlehide leather is employed for a great variety of purposes, the principal market is shoe manufacturing. Shoes alone consume from 85 per cent to 90 per cent of all cattlehide leather produced in the United States. Since 1929 no other single market such as luggage, belting, upholstery, etc., has accounted for more than 3 per cent of the cattlehide leather output." Merrill A. Watson, *Economics of Cattlehide Leather Tanning*, Chicago: Rumpf Publishing Co., 1950, p. 110.

[2]From data given by Watson, *ibid.*, pp. 115 and 118, we can roughly calculate that the percentage of leather shoes containing either rubber composition soles or fabric uppers rose from about 10 per cent in 1929 to about 25 per cent in 1940. Watson states that "shoe manufacturers are continuously searching for materials for footwear which meet the requirements of price and market suitability. This general policy is restricted only by the customary preference of the consumer for such traditional materials as leather." Nonetheless, Watson concludes that "leather is still the most important material used in the manufacture of footwear." (Quotations from p. 118.)

which could generate values of manufacturers' leather receipts. Various time paths resulted, depending upon the numerical values assigned to the four parameters r_s, r_l, m_l, and m_u.

This subsystem was simulated using a large number of values for these parameters until that set of values was found which minimized the sum of $[\hat{L}(t) - L(t)]^2$ from January, 1930 through December, 1940,[1] where $\hat{L}(t)$ is the time path for manufacturers' leather receipts and $L(t)$ is the observed time path. In this manner, the best values found for these parameters were:

r_s = .623 per month

r_l = .910 per month

m_l = \$0.00 per pair

m_u = \$1.41 per pair

These were the values used in Model II.

3.6. Tanners' Behavior

The major economic variables at the tanners' sector are the selling price of leather, the production of leather, and the receipts of hides. The technology of leather tanning is such that there is not necessarily a rigid cycle by which hides emerge as finished leather a definite length of time after they are entered into the tanning process. It is completely feasible for the tanning process to be interrupted in the middle, and for semitanned leather to be held indefinitely "in the crust" as in-process inventory. Thus, leather production by tanners must be broken down into two separate decision variables: hide wettings (the entering of hides

---

[1]Numerical methods had to be used to find the appropriate parameter values. In addition to throwing successively finer grids over the parameter space to explore more intensively those areas which seemed to contain relative minimum points of the criterion function, various modifications of the method of steepest descent were used. An early and fairly complete exposition of the latter method can be found in G.E.P. Box and K.B. Wilson, "On the Experimental Attainment of Optimum Conditions," *Journal of the Royal Statistical Society, Series B (Methodological)*, Vol. 13 (1951), pp. 1-45.

into the tanning process), and production of finished leather (the completion of the tanning process).

A further complication which first enters our models at the tanners' level is the desirability of differentiating various kinds of hides depending upon their source. There are three sources of hides to be considered: packer hides (which arise strictly as by-products of meat packing), country hides (the price sensitive component of the domestic hide supply), and imported hides (which, for American markets, are entirely free of the by-product character and whose supply is extremely price sensitive). Technologically, the hides from all three sources are completely interchangeable with respect to their usability in the production of leather, so it is not necessary to divide the tanners' hide stocks or production flows according to hide source. However, different types of mechanisms determine the tanners' placement of hide orders with the various sources.

In attempting to obtain behavioral mechanisms explaining the major economic variables at the tanners' level, we found that not enough information was available. Mrs. Mack's analysis was only adequate to formulate implications about tanners' behavior in the form of functional dependencies. For the tanners' sector, it was necessary to rely upon the procedures of traditional aggregate econometrics, formulating regression equations to "explain" the tanners' behavior in terms of those variables which our theory indicated were most important.

Following Mrs. Mack's lead, [1] our models assume that domestic hides are received in the same month as they are ordered, while imported hides are received two months later. Hence:

(46) $$R^I(t) = Q^I(t - 2)$$

(47) $$R^c(t) = Q^c(t)$$

(48) $$R^P(t) = Q^P(t)$$

(49) $$R(t) = R^P(t) + R^c(t) + R^I(t)$$

---

[1]Mack, *op. cit.*, p. 176.

Mrs. Mack hypothesizes[1] that leather prices are largely determined by current and recent hide prices. A large number of regression equations were explored. All of these explained leather prices as a function of a variety of current and lagged hide prices, lagged leather prices, an exogenous seasonal factor, tanners' leather shipments, tanners' finished leather stocks, and the turnover of tanners' finished leather stocks. The most satisfactory regression equation, and the one incorporated in Model II, is:

$$(50) \quad Lp(t) = C_{0,50} + C_{1,50}Lp(t-1) \\ + C_{2,50}Hp(t) + C_{3,50}Hp(t-1)$$

The regression coefficients in equation (50) are all statistically significant at the 5 per cent level or better. Single equation least squares techniques produced the following estimates of the regression coefficients and (in parentheses) the number of times each coefficient exceeds its standard error:

$C_{0,50} = .263$

$C_{1,50} = .916 \ (46.8)$

$C_{2,50} = .566 \ (13.8)$

$C_{3,50} = -.459 \ (9.7)$

The multiple correlation coefficient adjusted for degrees of freedom is .99.

Mrs. Mack reports[2] that tanners' production decisions depend upon: (a) the volume of shoe production, translated into leather requirements; (b) the volume of incoming orders for leather, which, in Model II, is the same as leather shipments; (c) inventories, which are watched to see that they are not backing up or spooling out too fast; and (d) inventories, which are watched to see that they are neither too large nor too small relative to shipments. Mrs. Mack's discussion and her timing and amplitude comparisons[3] lead to these hypotheses: (a) finished leather production

---

[1]*Ibid.*, pp. 180-184.
[2]*Ibid.*, p. 186.
[3]*Ibid.*, pp. 186-187.

depends upon finished leather production last month and the turnover rate of tanners' finished leather stocks last month; and (b) hide wettings depend upon hide wettings last month, the current turnover rate of tanners' finished leather stocks, and the change in tanners' finished leather stocks over the past five months. A large number of regression equations explaining finished leather production and hide wettings as functions of these variables as well as of exogenous seasonal factors were tried. The most satisfactory of these equations were incorporated in Model II:

$$(51)\ X(t) = C_{0,51} + C_{1,51}X(t-1)$$
$$+ C_{2,51}\frac{L(t-1)}{\frac{1}{2}[J^L(t-2) + J^L(t-1)]} + C_{3,51}W(t-1) + C_{4,51}M_X(t)$$

and

$$(52)\ W(t) = C_{0,52} + C_{1,52}W(t-1) + C_{2,52}\frac{L(t)}{\frac{1}{2}[J^L(t-1) + J^L(t)]}$$
$$+ C_{3,52}\frac{J^L(t-1) - J^L(t-6)}{5} + C_{4,52}M_W(t)$$

All the coefficients in equations (51) and (52) are statistically significant at the 5 per cent level or better. Single equation least squares estimation yielded the following estimates of the regression coefficients and (in parentheses) the number of times each coefficient exceeds its standard error:

$$C_{0,51} = -1,010,000$$
$$C_{1,51} = .387\ (3.3)$$
$$C_{2,51} = 601,000\ (3.8)$$
$$C_{3,51} = .285\ (2.0)$$
$$C_{4,51} = 13,500\ (5.4)$$
$$C_{0,52} = -752,000$$
$$C_{1,52} = .468\ (9.6)$$
$$C_{2,52} = 974,000\ (10.8)$$
$$C_{3,52} = .159\ (2.4)$$
$$C_{4,52} = 11,100\ (4.4)$$

The multiple correlation coefficients adjusted for degrees of freedom are .92 for equation (51) and .95 for equation (52).

It is extremely difficult to obtain from Mrs. Mack's discussion[1] of tanners' ordering behavior any clearly formulated hypotheses concerning the determination of tanners' orders for hides from various sources. A large number of regression equations were tried to explain the various aspects of tanners' hide orders in terms of such variables as lagged hide orders, lagged hide receipts, various kinds of hide prices, changes in hide prices, margins between leather and hide prices, tanners' finished leather production, tanners' leather shipments, changes in tanners' leather shipments, turnover rates of tanners' finished leather stocks, hide wettings, and exogenous seasonal factors. We used the most satisfactory of these equations in Model II:

$$(53) \quad Q(t) = C_{0,53} + C_{1,53}Hp(t - 1) + C_{2,53}W(t) + C_{3,53}M_Q(t)$$

$$(54) \quad R^D(t) = C_{0,54} + C_{1,54}R^D(t - 1) + C_{2,54}Q(t) + C_{3,54}X(t - 1) + C_{4,54}W(t - 1) + C_{5,54}M_{R^D}(t)$$

and

$$(55) \quad R^P(t) = C_{0,55} + C_{1,55}R^D(t) + C_{2,55}W(t - 1) + C_{3,55}M_{R^P}(t)$$

All the coefficients in equations (53), (54), and (55) are statistically significant at the 5 per cent level or better. Single equation least squares techniques resulted in the following estimates of the regression coefficients and (in parentheses) the number of times each coefficient exceeds its standard error:

$$C_{0,53} = -991,000$$

$$C_{1,53} = -54,900 \ (3.9)$$

$$C_{2,53} = 1.20 \ (15.7)$$

$$C_{3,53} = 9,660 \ (4.9)$$

$$C_{0,54} = -135,000$$

$$C_{1,54} = .297 \ (4.7)$$

---

[1] *Ibid.*, pp. 205-215.

$$C_{2,54} = .544 \; (12.2)$$

$$C_{3,54} = .361 \; (3.0)$$

$$C_{4,54} = -.516 \; (3.7)$$

$$C_{5,54} = 3,920 \; (2.8)$$

$$C_{0,55} = 267,000$$

$$C_{1,55} = .757 \; (23.0)$$

$$C_{2,55} = -.0818 \; (2.7)$$

$$C_{3,55} = -3,070 \; (2.9)$$

The multiple correlation coefficients adjusted for degrees of freedom are .86 for equation (53), .89 for equation (54), and .92 for equation (55).

The following inventory identities complete our specification of the tanners' sector for Model II:

(56) $$J^H(t) = J^H(t-1) + R(t) - W(t)$$

(57) $$J^I(t) = J^I(t-1) + W(t) - X(t)$$

and

(58) $$J^L(t) = J^L(t-1) + X(t) - L(t)$$

3.7. Hide Dealers' Selling Prices

The only interaction between the hide dealers' sector and other levels of the shoe, leather, hide sequence that our models explain is the pricing behavior of hide dealers. Since the various sources of hides differ considerably among themselves in regard to the sensitivity of their supply functions to changes in selling price, the models consider not only average hide prices but also the prices of packer hides, country hides, and imported hides. As was the case with the tanners' sector, the information that Mrs. Mack has provided about the hide dealers' activities is not adequate to yield behavioral mechanisms describing their pricing behavior. Hence, we must once again operate only at the aggregate sector level of "explanation," and look for suitable regression equations determining hide prices.

To explain average hide prices, Mrs. Mack suggests[1] a linear regression equation with tanners' leather shipments, the stock-location ratio,[2] and factory shoe price as the independent variables. Several regression equations were fitted expressing the dependence of average hide prices not only upon these variables but also upon tanners' hide receipts, hide wettings, finished leather production, lagged hide prices, stocks of hides held by hide dealers, and an exogenous seasonal factor. The most satisfactory equation was incorporated into Model II:

$$(59) \quad Hp(t) = C_{0,59} + $$
$$C_{1,59} \frac{G(t-1) + G(t) + J^I(t-1) + J^I(t) + J^H(t-1) + J^H(t)}{J^L(t-1) + J^L(t) + \Gamma(t-1) + \Gamma(t)}$$
$$+ C_{2,59} Fp(t) + C_{3,59} X(t) + C_{4,59} W(t)$$

All of the coefficients in equation (59) are statistically significant at the 5 per cent level or better. Single equation least squares estimates produced the following results for the estimates of the regression coefficients and (in parentheses) the number of times each coefficient exceeds its standard error:

$$C_{0,59} = -6.19$$
$$C_{1,59} = 1.40 \ (3.9)$$
$$C_{2,59} = 2.02 \ (8.1)$$
$$C_{3,59} = .183 \times 10^{-5} \ (2.6)$$
$$C_{4,59} = .183 \times 10^{-5} \ (2.2)$$

The multiple correlation coefficient adjusted for degrees of freedom was .86.

Mrs. Mack presents no specific hypotheses explaining the prices of packer hides, country hides, and imported hides separately. We explored numerous regression equations expressing

---

[1] *Ibid.*, pp. 224-229.

[2] "The stock-location ratio is the ratio of leather in the hands of leathergoods manufacturers and of raw and in-process hides in the hands of tanners — stocks of buyers — to finished leather in the hands of tanners and hides in the hands of packers, butchers, and hide dealers — stocks of sellers." *Ibid.*, pp. 223-224.

packer hide prices, imported hide prices, and the hide price ratio as functions of various kinds of orders for and receipts of hides by tanners, various current and lagged hide prices, stocks of hides held by hide dealers, and exogenous seasonal factors. The most satisfactory of these regression equations were used in Model II:

$$(60) \quad Hp^R(t) = C_{0,60} + C_{1,60}Hp^R(t-1) + C_{2,60}Hp(t) \\ + C_{3,60}[R^c(t-2) + R^I(t-2)] + C_{4,60}M_{Hp^R}(t)$$

$$(61) \quad Hp^P(t) = C_{0,61} + C_{1,61}\frac{\Gamma(t-1) + \Gamma(t)}{2} + C_{2,61}Hp(t) \\ + C_{3,61}Hp^R(t)$$

and

$$(62) \quad Hp^I(t) = C_{0,62} + C_{1,62}Q^I(t) + C_{2,62}Hp(t) + C_{3,62}Hp^R(t)$$

All the regression coefficients in equations (60), (61), and (62) are statistically significant at the 5 per cent level or better. Single equation least squares techniques yielded the following estimates of the coefficients and (in parentheses) the number of times each coefficient exceeds its standard error:

$C_{0,60} = -.0393$

$C_{1,60} = .534 \ (819)$

$C_{2,60} = -.00965 \ (2.8)$

$C_{3,60} = .563 \times 10^{-7} \ (2.2)$

$C_{4,60} = .00427 \ (6.9)$

$C_{0,61} = .0450$

$C_{1,61} = .202 \times 10^{-8} \ (2.9)$

$C_{2,61} = .0244 \ (48.7)$

$C_{3,61} = -.0588 \ (7.1)$

$C_{0,62} = -.0731$

$C_{1,62} = -.144 \times 10^{-7} \ (2.4)$

$C_{2,62} = .0240 \ (35.5)$

$C_{3,62} = .0980 \ (10.3)$

The multiple correlation coefficients adjusted for degrees of freedom are .87 for equation (60), .98 for equation (61), and .96 for equation (62).

3.8. Model IIE

Model II is a *process model* of the shoe, leather, hide sequence, i.e., a model in which after the initial period the values of lagged endogenous variables appearing in its relations are the values which were generated by the model and not the actual values assumed by these variables. Since a process model asserts a great deal about the nature of the world, there is a strong likelihood that in some respects it is an incorrect description of the reality it is intended to portray. A process model may misspecify some of the mechanisms it contains, leading to values of the endogenous variables which differ from their actual values to some extent. As such a model unfolds through time, the "past history" at the start of each period does not provide the same "jumping-off point" as that from which the world actually started. It is thus possible that small errors arising from slight misspecifications in the process model can accumulate over time until the paths followed by the endogenous variables bear no resemblance to the observed time paths.

As a check to see whether such an accumulation of errors does significantly distort the time paths generated by Model II, Model IIE was also formulated. The latter is a *one-period-change* model of the shoe, leather, hide sequence incorporating the same mechanisms as Model II. The relations in Model IIE are exactly the same as the relations in Model II, the only difference being that in simulating Model IIE, lagged endogenous variables are always replaced by their observed values,[1] whereas in simulating Model II lagged endogenous variables are replaced by the values previously generated for them by the model.

---

[1] The single exception is retailers' orders for shoes. Since no actual data concerning retailers' orders from 1930-1940 is available, it is impossible to correct lagged values of this set of variables.

3.9. Nature of the Models

The specific mechanisms contained in Models II and IIE have now been completely presented. Careful examination reveals that the nature of our models is descriptive rather than normative. Our models are intended to describe the decision-rules which determine the actions of individual firms. It was possible to formulate behavioral mechanisms to explain retailers' selling price, sales, and purchases and manufacturers' production and purchases. Lack of information required the models to provide sector level regression equations for the determination of consumers' purchases, manufacturers' selling price, tanners' selling price, production, and purchases, and hide dealers' selling price.

To the extent that computer models can be formulated entirely in terms of behavioral mechanisms describing the processes by which individual firms form their expectations and carry out their actions, there is no need to introduce the concept of profit maximization. The proposition that business firms maximize profits is not a derived theorem in the neoclassical theory of the firm, but rather it is a fundamental postulate required by that theory to obtain propositions concerning the selling price and production of firms. When computer models of individual firms are based upon the actual decision-making processes which determine the firms' behavior, and when these behavioral mechanisms are obtained by direct observation of the firms, no additional normative assumptions need be invoked in order to derive propositions concerning the firms' selling price and production variables. An independent test of the proposition that firms maximize profits is then possible for such a model.

Although computer models formalizing a behavioral theory of the firm arise originally as descriptive models, they have important normative implications. Such models must describe in great detail the information and mechanisms determining the behavior of individual firms. The models themselves can be used as laboratory situations. Changes can be introduced in the informational pattern, the anticipations rules, and the decision processes contained in the model, and the effects of these changes on the behavior of the system can be found by simulating the resulting system. In this way, the management of a firm can determine the changes necessary in the behavioral mechanisms to produce "optimal" behavior according to whatever goals they hold, whether these goals be profit maximization, sales maximization, cost minimization, or anything else.

The extent to which Models II and IIE can be considered explanations of observed behavior in the shoe, leather, hide sequence is considered in Chapter 5, following a discussion in Chapter 4 of the way these models were simulated.

Computer Realization of the
Shoe, Leather, Hide Models

4.1. Monthly Computational Flow

In Chapter 3 we described the mechanisms contained in our shoe, leather, hide models in an order which was intended to facilitate understanding the nature of our models and the sources of the hypotheses we used in formulating them. This is not the most efficient order for listing these relations, however, when we are interested in tracing out the time paths generated by the models. In order to see the way in which a digital computer would simulate our models, we now shall restate the mechanisms in an efficient sequence for determining the values of all the endogenous variables each month. With this particular ordering, our models become strictly recursive systems, with the convenient feature that the current values of all the endogenous variables can be calculated one variable at a time in sequence, without our ever having to solve any sets of simultaneous equations.

Most of the relations appearing in the monthly computational flow listing below were already described in Chapter 3. A few new relations are first introduced here; however, these are either definitional identities or constraints which insure that stocks, flows, and prices are nonnegative.[1]

For $\tau = 0, 1, \cdots 8$:

(9) $S_{t-1}(t + \tau) =$

$$\alpha S(t + \tau - 12) \; \frac{S(t - 1) + S(t - 2) + S(t - 3)}{S(t - 13) + S(t - 14) + S(t - 15)}$$

$$+ (1 - \alpha)S(t + \tau - 12)$$

In case $S(t - 13) + S(t - 14) + S(t - 15) = 0$, then take

$$S_{t-1}(t + \tau) = S(t + \tau - 12)$$

(15) $\qquad h^{*}_{t-1}(t) = S_{t-1}(t) + C_{h*}$

(16) $\Omega^0(t) = h^{*}_{t-1}(t) - [H(t - 1) + \Omega^1(t - 1) + \Omega^2(t - 2)$

$$+ \Omega^3(t - 3)],$$

subject to $\Omega^0(t) \geq 0$

(17) $\qquad h^{*}_{t-1}(t + 1) = S_{t-1}(t + 1) + C_{h*}$

(18) $H_{t-1}(t) = H(t - 1) + \Omega^0(t) + \Omega^1(t - 1) + \Omega^2(t - 2)$

$$+ \Omega^3(t - 3) - S_{t-1}(t)$$

(19) $\quad \Omega^1(t) = h^{*}_{t-1}(t + 1) - [H_{t-1}(t) + \Omega^2(t - 1) + \Omega^3(t - 2)],$

subject to $\Omega^1(t) \geq 0$

(20) $\quad \Omega^2(t) = 0$ for $t =$ Jan., Feb., Apr., May, June, July,

Aug., Oct., Nov., Dec.

(22) $H_{t-1}(t + 1) = H_{t-1}(t) + \Omega^1(t) + \Omega^2(t - 1) + \Omega^3(t - 2)$

$$- S_{t-1}(t + 1) \text{ for } t = \text{Mar., June, Sept., Dec.}$$

(23) $\quad h^{*}_{t-1}(t + 2) = S_{t-1}(t + 2) + C_{h*}$ for $t =$ Mar., Sept.

(24) $\Omega^2(t) = h^{*}_{t-1}(t + 2) - [H_{t-1}(t + 1) + \Omega^3(t - 1)]$

$$+ \sum_{\tau=3}^{5} S_{t-1}(t + \tau) \qquad\qquad \text{for } t = \text{Mar., Sept.,}$$

subject to $\Omega^2(t) \geq 0$

(21) $\qquad \Omega^3(t) = 0 \qquad\qquad$ for $t =$ Jan., Feb., Mar., Apr., May,

July, Aug., Sept., Oct., Nov.

---

[1]The actual forms of the constraints which insure nonnegative prices are that in any month no price can increase by more than 100 per cent or decrease by more than 50 per cent. In addition to keeping prices positive, these constraints also rule out extremely rapid price changes, increasing the stability of the models.

(28) $H_{t-1}(t+2) = H_{t-1}(t+1) + \Omega^3(t-1) - S_{t-1}(t+2)$
$$\text{for } t = \text{June, Dec.}$$

(29) $h^*_{t-1}(t+3) = S_{t-1}(t+3) + C_{h^*}$ for t = June, Dec.

(27) $\nu = \dfrac{Hp(t-1) - Hp(t-4)}{Hp(t-4)}$ for t = June, Dec.,

subject to $\nu \geq 0$

(26) $\mu = \frac{1}{3}(1 - \nu) + \nu$ for t = June, Dec.,

subject to $\mu \leq 1$

(25) $\Omega^3(t) = h^*_{t-1}(t+3) - H_{t-1}(t+2) - S_{t-1}(t+3)$
$$+ \mu \sum_{\tau=3}^{8} S_{t-1}(t+\tau) \qquad \text{for } t = \text{June, Dec.,}$$

subject to $\Omega^3(t) \geq 0$

(10) $\Sigma(t) = \Omega^0(t) + \Omega^1(t-1) + \Omega^2(t-2) + \Omega^3(t-3)$

(33) $Fp(t) = C_{0,33} + C_{1,33} Bls(t-1) + C_{2,33} Dpi(t-1)$
$$+ C_{3,33}[Lp(t-1) + Lp(t-2) + \cdots + Lp(t-6)] \div 6,$$

subject to $\frac{1}{2}Fp(t-1) \leq Fp(t) \leq 2Fp(t-1)$

(51) $X(t) = C_{0,51} + C_{1,51}X(t-1)$
$$+ C_{2,51}\frac{L(t-1)}{\frac{1}{2}[J^L(t-2) + J^L(t-1)]} + C_{3,51}W(t-1)$$
$$+ C_{4,51}M_X(t),$$

subject to $0 \leq X(t) \leq J^l(t-1)$

(32) $P(t) = \frac{1}{4}[\Omega^3(t-3) + \Omega^3(t-2) + \Omega^3(t-1) + \Omega^3(t)]$
$$+ \frac{1}{3}[\Omega^2(t-2) + \Omega^2(t-1) + \Omega^2(t)]$$
$$+ \frac{1}{2}[\Omega^1(t-1) + \Omega^1(t)] + \Omega^0(t),$$

subject to $0 \leq P(t) \geq \Sigma(t) - G^s(t-1)$

(43) $Lp_{\min}(t) = \min[Lp(t-1), Lp(t-2), \cdots, Lp(t-6)]$

(44) $\rho^* = \left(\dfrac{1}{2}\right)\dfrac{Hp(t-1) - Hp(t-4)}{Hp(t-4)}$
$$+ \left(\dfrac{1}{2}\right)\dfrac{Lp(t-1) - Lp_{\min}(t)}{Lp_{\min}(t)}$$

(41) $\rho = 0$ if $Fp(t-1) - \lambda Lp(t-1) \leq m_l$
$\rho = 1$ if $Fp(t-1) - \lambda Lp(t-1) \geq m_u$

If $m_l < Fp(t - 1) - \lambda Lp(t - 1) < m_u$, then:

(42) $\qquad\qquad \rho = 0$ if $P(t) \leq P(t - 12)$

If $m_l < Fp(t - 1) - \lambda Lp(t - 1) < m_u$ and $P(t) > P(t - 12)$, then:

$$\rho = \rho^* \qquad\qquad \text{if} \quad 0 \leq \rho^* \leq 1$$

(45) $\qquad\qquad \rho = 0 \qquad\qquad\quad\, \text{if} \quad \rho^* < 0$

$$\rho = 1 \qquad\qquad\quad\, \text{if} \quad \rho^* > 1$$

(40) $L(t) = (1 - \rho)\left[\left(1 + \dfrac{1}{r_l}\right) \lambda P(t) - G(t - 1)\right]$
$$+ \rho\left[\left(1 + \dfrac{1}{r_s}\right) \lambda P(t) - G(t - 1)\right],$$

subject to

$$0 \leq L(t) \geq \lambda P(t) - G(t - 1)$$

and

$$L(t) \leq J^L(t - 1)$$

If necessary, modify the previously calculated values for $P(t)$ and $\Sigma(t)$ to insure that

$$P(t) \leq \frac{G(t - 1) + L(t)}{\lambda}$$

and

$$\Sigma(t) \leq G^s(t - 1) + P(t)$$
$$G^s(t) = G^s(t - 1) + P(t) - \Sigma(t)$$

(30) $\qquad\quad G(t) = G(t - 1) + L(t) - \lambda P(t)$

(58) $\qquad\quad J^L(t) = J^L(t - 1) + X(t) - L(t)$

(52) $W(t) = C_{0,52} + C_{1,52} W(t - 1)$
$$+ C_{2,52} \frac{L(t)}{\frac{1}{2}[J^L(t - 1) + J^L(t)]}$$
$$+ C_{3,52} \frac{J^L(t - 1) - J^L(t - 6)}{5} + C_{4,52} M_W(t),$$

subject to

$$0 \leq W(t) \leq J^H(t - 1)$$

(57) $\qquad\qquad J^I(t) = J^I(t - 1) + W(t) - X(t)$

(53) $Q(t) = C_{0,53} + C_{1,53} Hp(t-1) + C_{2,53}W(t) + C_{3,53}M_Q(t),$

subject to $Q(t) \geq 0$

(54) $R^D(t) = C_{0,54} + C_{1,54}R^D(t-1) + C_{2,54}Q(t) + C_{3,54}X(t-1)$
$\qquad + C_{4,54}W(t-1) + C_{5,54}M_{R^D}(t),$

subject to $R^D(t) \geq 0$

(46) $\qquad\qquad\qquad R^I(t) = Q^I(t-2)$

In case $R^D(t) + R^I(t) < 0$, then set

$$R^D(t) = -R^I(t)$$
$$Q^I(t) = Q(t) - R^D(t)$$
$$R(t) = R^D(t) + R^I(t)$$

(56) $J^H(t) = J^H(t-1) + R(t) - W(t)$

(55) $R^P(t) = C_{0,55} + C_{1,55}R^D(t) + C_{2,55}W(t-1) + C_{3,55}M_{R^P}(t),$

subject to

$$0 \leq R^P(t) \leq R^D(t)$$
$$R^C(t) = R^D(t) - R^P(t)$$

(6) $Fp^*(t) = [H(t-1)Fp^*(t-1) + \Omega^0(t)Fp(t)$
$\qquad + \Omega^1(t-1)Fp(t-1) + \Omega^2(t-2)Fp(t-2)$
$\qquad + \Omega^3(t-3)Fp(t-3)] \div [\Sigma(t) + H(t-1)]$

(5) $\qquad\qquad Rp(t) = \dfrac{Fp^*(t)}{1 - Rpmu},$

subject to

$$\tfrac{1}{2}Rp(t-1) \leq Rp(t) \leq 2Rp(t-1)$$

(3) $\qquad [SRp](t) = C_{0,3} + C_{1,3}Dpi(t) + C_{2,3}M_{[SRp]}(t),$

subject to

$$0 \leq [SRp](t) \leq [H(t-1) + \Sigma(t)] Rp(t)$$

(7) $\qquad\qquad S(t) = [SRp](t) \div Rp(t),$

subject to $S(t) \leq H(t-1) + \Sigma(t)$

(11) $\qquad\qquad H(t) = H(t-1) + \Sigma(t) - S(t)$

(59) $Hp(t) = C_{0,59} +$

$$C_{1,59} \frac{G(t-1) + G(t) + J^I(t-1) + J^I(t) + J^H(t-1) + J^H(t)}{J^L(t-1) + J^L(t) + \Gamma(t-1) + \Gamma(t)}$$
$$+ C_{2,59}Fp(t) + C_{3,59}X(t) + C_{4,59}W(t),$$

subject to

$$\tfrac{1}{2}Hp(t-1) \leq Hp(t) \leq 2Hp(t-1)$$

(60) $Hp^R(t) = C_{0,60} + C_{1,60}Hp^R(t-1) + C_{2,60}Hp(t)$
$$+ C_{3,60}[R^C(t-2) + R^I(t-2)] + C_{4,60}M_{Hp^R}(t),$$

subject to

$$\tfrac{1}{4}Hp^R(t-1) \leq Hp^R(t) \leq 4Hp^R(t-1)$$

(61) $Hp^P(t) = C_{0,61} + C_{1,61} \dfrac{\Gamma(t-1) + \Gamma(t)}{2}$
$$+ C_{2,61}Hp(t) + C_{3,61}Hp^R(t),$$

subject to

$$\tfrac{1}{2}Hp^P(t-1) \leq Hp^P(t) \leq 2Hp^P(t-1)$$

(62) $Hp^I(t) = C_{0,62} + C_{1,62}Q^I(t) + C_{2,62}Hp(t) + C_{3,62}Hp^R(t),$

subject to

$$\tfrac{1}{2}Hp^I(t-1) \leq Hp^I(t) \leq 2Hp^I(t-1)$$

(50) $Lp(t) = C_{0,50} + C_{1,50}Lp(t-1) + C_{2,50}Hp(t)$
$$+ C_{3,50}Hp(t-1),$$

subject to

$$\tfrac{1}{2}Lp(t-1) \leq Lp(t) \leq 2Lp(t-1)$$

4.2. Programming and Simulation

Models II and IIE were programmed for and simulated on the IBM 650 RAMAC electronic digital computer at the Carnegie Institute of Technology Computation Center. The coding was mainly done using a general scientific compiler developed at Carnegie Tech.[1] The storage capacity of the drum and cores was inadequate, so the random access (disk) memory was used as

---

[1]A. J. Perlis, J. W. Smith, and H. R. Van Zoeren, *Internal Translator (IT), A Compiler for the 650*, 650 Library Program, File Number 2.1.001, IBM, 1957.

an integral part of the simulation. Each model was programmed in five segments, these being stored on disks and called onto the drum as needed. The program segments were:

Segment 1: Beginning.

Segment 2: Compute current values of the endogenous variables.

Segment 3: Compute current values of the endogenous variables (continued).

Segment 4: Write current values of the endogenous variables on disks and update past history.

Segment 5: Output time paths generated by model.

The first and the fifth segments were each executed only once, at the beginning and end of the simulation runs. The second, third, and fourth segments were executed once for each month of the simulation. The actual calculations were done in the second and third segments, corresponding to the equations shown above in Section 4.1. The fourth segment performs only housekeeping operations.

The values of all the parameters and the current values of each time series variable and as many past values as are required by the models were assigned fixed drum locations (i.e., in the Internal Translator coding, they were called specific I, Y, and C variables). At the start of the simulation, the values of all parameters, the required past history, and the current values of the exogenous variables were read onto the drum, in Segment 1. For Model IIE, Segment 1 also read the actual values for all the endogenous variables from 1930–1940 onto the disks.[1] Segments 2 and 3 then calculated the January, 1930 values of all the time series generated by the model. Segment 4 transferred these calculated values for January, 1930 to the disks for storage and then updated the past history. In Model II, this updating was done using the values generated by the model for January, 1930 (e.g., shoe sales in month $t - 1$, which initially were the actual shoe sales for Decem-

---

[1]Except for retailers' orders of shoes, where actual data are lacking.

ber, 1929, would be set equal to the calculated shoe sales for January, 1930). In Model IIE, this updating was done using the actual values of the endogenous variables[1] (which were stored on disks by Segment 1). After all the relevant history had been updated, the program returned to Segment 2, to begin calculating the time series values for February, 1930.

In this manner, every "month" of the simulation generates the current values of each of the model's endogenous variables. These "current" values are transferred to the disks, where the endogenous variables are stored as time series. When the simulation has finished the final month, the time paths generated by the model for the entire period covered are punched out as complete time series, one variable at a time.

The program for each model consists of approximately six thousand machine language instructions. It takes about five minutes to read the program into the computer and store it on disks. The output of twenty-seven time series for eleven years requires about eight minutes. Each month can be simulated in one minute with Model II and in one and one-quarter minutes with Model IIE.[2] Thus, if run in a single session (which they need not be, since the programs were written to be interruptible and restartable), the simulation of Model II for eleven years requires approximately two and one-half hours and the simulation of Model IIE for eleven years requires approximately three hours of time on our IBM 650 RAMAC.

Special input and output routines were written which allowed us to have the twelve monthly values for a year for a variable on a single IBM punch card. Although this restricted us to an accuracy of at most four significant digits, it greatly facilitated the preparation and interpretation of the enormous amounts of monthly time series data required in our research.

---

[1]Again, retailers' orders for shoes had to be treated as an exception. We were forced to use the values generated by Model IIE as the past history for this set of variables.

[2]Model IIE requires the additional time for transferring from disks to drum the actual values of the endogenous variables at the end of each "month."

CHAPTER 5

Results of the Simulation Runs

5.1. Monthly Time Paths Generated by Models II and IIE

The simulation runs for both Models II and IIE generate time paths for the endogenous variables which, although not in complete agreement with the observed time paths, indicate that our models may incorporate some of the mechanisms which determined behavior in the shoe, leather, hide sequence. Charts 1 through 22 compare the values generated by our models for the eleven major endogenous variables[1] with the actual values. On a month-by-month comparison, Model IIE generally seems to perform better than Model II. Both models produce time paths which fluctuate around the observed values. For most variables, the amplitude of the oscillations is greater for Model IIE than

---

[1]Altogether, there are twenty-seven endogenous variables in each model for which actual data for 1930-1940 are available. To avoid excessive boredom for the reader, analysis of the results is focused upon the most important variables, prices and physical flows. Inventories have all been omitted since they are determined by physical inflows and outflows, which are all included. The dollar volume of retail shoe sales is omitted, since it is determined by retail shoe price and retail shoe sales in pairs, both of which are included. Finally, prices and shipments pertaining to the classification of hides by source into packer hides, country hides, and imported hides were omitted, since at the sector level aggregate hide prices and flows are more important. The endogenous variables actually considered are the following eleven: retail shoe price, factory shoe price, leather price, average hide price, retail pair shoe sales, retailers' shoe receipts, shoe production, manufacturers' leather receipts, finished leather production, hide wettings, and tanners' receipts of all hides.

for the actuals, with Model II having the largest amplitude. However, none of the time paths for either model seems to be either explosive or overly damped.

Charts 1 and 2 compare the values of retail shoe price determined by Models II and IIE with actual values. The time paths traced out by both models for this variable are not at all unreasonable, although both calculated series seem to lag slightly behind changes in the observed series. The sharp fluctuations in the values generated for retailers' shoe orders in both models impart a ratchet-like quality to the time paths for retail shoe price, an effect which is especially pronounced in Model II.

The pictures for factory shoe price, Charts 3 and 4, show that Model IIE traces out a time path which is in extremely close agreement with the observed time path. Model II also performs well, although its generated values oscillate slightly around the actual values.

Charts 5 and 6 tell a similar story for leather price. Both Models II and IIE behave fairly well, although not quite as well as they did for factory shoe price.

The findings are also similar for average hide price, Charts 7 and 8. The time paths of both Models II and IIE are reasonably on course with the observed values, although Model II shows even wider fluctuations about the actuals than for the preceding prices.

Both models perform very well in reproducing the physical volume of retail shoe sales, as Charts 9 and 10 show.

Retailers' receipts of shoes, Charts 11 and 12, is the first variable for which the models produce undeniably bad results. Both models generate time paths for retailers' shoe receipts that fluctuate far more than the actuals. These time paths are characterized by marked alternations of zeros and extremely high values, with the extremes reached by Model II higher than those achieved by Model IIE. However, there is no explosive tendency apparent in the retailers' shoe receipts of either model.

The behavior of the models is similarly bad for manufacturers' shoe production, shown on Charts 13 and 14. Both shoe production and retailers' shoe receipts could be expected to show similar characteristics, since both largely reflect the pattern of retailers' orders for shoes (one important endogenous variable for which no observed data exist).

These unfortunate results also extend to manufacturers' receipts of leather, Charts 15 and 16. The extreme oscillations in the models' values for leather receipts are actually induced by errors present in the shoe production series. Again, however, there seems to be no overall tendency towards explosive behavior.

The outlook begins to brighten with tanners' finished leather production, pictured in Charts 17 and 18. The comparison of generated and actual time paths is extremely good for Model IIE and only moderately good for Model II, the latter showing large fluctuations around what seems to be the right general level.

The comparisons for tanners' hide wettings, Charts 19 and 20, look a little less good. Model IIE does better than Model II, but both produce time paths which oscillate around the actual values.

Finally, Charts 21 and 22 show tanners' receipts of all hides. Model IIE performs reasonably well for this variable, but the behavior of Model II is only mediocre. However, both models yield time paths which fluctuate about the actual values.

5.2. Interpretations of These Results

Since process models can accumulate errors from period to period through the lagged endogenous variables while one-period-change models are free from this source of disturbance, it would be expected on a priori grounds that the output from Model IIE would bear a closer resemblance to reality than the time paths generated by Model II. Charts 1 through 22 generally showed that this expectation was fulfilled.

Although for some variables the models behaved reasonably well, the over-all monthly results do not reveal an adequate description of all aggregate variables in the shoe, leather, hide sequence. In particular, the models perform badly for three major variables: retailers' receipts of shoes, manufacturers' production of shoes, and manufacturers' receipts of leather. The models also impart certain peculiarities into the generated series for retail shoe price.

The poor results for these four important endogenous variables all stem from difficulties arising in the retailers' rules for ordering shoes. These rules describe the processes which determine the shoe orders placed by a typical retailer. The retailers base their anticipations regarding future sales upon past sales experience. The retailers determine a "minimum desired" inventory level for the present and future according to their sales forecasts. Taking into account the expected depletion of stocks due to anticipated future sales, retailers always order at least enough shoes to attain these "minimum desired" levels. Twice each season retailers place long-term delivery orders to obtain the bulk of their anticipated seasonal needs.

The receipts of shoes by retailers is determined by the placement of orders, each order resulting in a shipment a given number of months later. Retail selling price depends only upon the orders placed by retailers and the factory shoe price prevailing when the order was placed. Manufacturers' shoe production occurs only as a result of retailers' orders. Manufacturers' leather purchases are determined by their own complex behavioral mechanism, a set of processes critically affected by shoe production. Through shoe production, retailers' orders for shoes produce a strong impact upon manufacturers' leather receipts.

The features of the generated time paths for retail shoe price, retailers' shoe receipts, manufacturers' shoe production, and manufacturers' leather receipts which make them appear ludicrous at the aggregate sector level could be realistic images of the patterns these variables might assume for individual firms. At a single firm level, selling prices may very well display ratchet-like patterns; and physical flows, because of economic lot size considerations, may very well consist of strings of zeros interrupted by an occasional high value. However, when these variables for individual firms are averaged or added over all retailers or all manufacturers to produce the corresponding sector-wide values, the high values of some firms cancel the low values of other firms, resulting in a pattern of aggregate values much more stable than the patterns displayed by individual firms.

In Chapter 3, our goal was to explore the extent to which a sector model of the shoe, leather, hide sequence consisting of behavior mechanisms describing the operations of a typical firm in each sector could generate the observed aggregate behavior in these industries. It appears that the four major endogenous variables which behave most poorly in the models are the only ones for which it was possible to formulate behavioral mechanisms to explain their determination. All the other major endogenous variables are generated either by regression equations or by identities. Herein lies the root of the difficulties.

Evidence introduced below indicates that the behavioral mechanisms of our models may be descriptions of the ways in which individual retailers and manufacturers act. However, even if every retailer and every manufacturer behaved according to the same mechanisms, differences exist in the *timing* of these mechanisms for the individual firms (e.g., selling seasons and delivery lead times may vary widely among firms) and the *distribution* of inventories among the individual firms (e.g., even though the aggregate level of retailers' inventories is high, some retailers may have low inventories). Because of these differences, the aggregate sector variables do not satisfy the same functional forms as the individual firm's behavior mechanisms.[1]

---

[1] Excellent discussions of the importance of timing and distribution in connection with the aggregation problem can be found in:

    (a) H. Theil, *Linear Aggregation of Economic Relations*, Amsterdam: North-Holland Publishing Company, 1954;

    (b) Franco Modigliani, "Business Reasons for Holding Inventories and Their Macro-Economic Implications," *Problems in Capital Formation*, Studies in Income and Wealth, Vol. 19, New York: National Bureau of Economic Research, 1957, pp. 495-506;

    (c) Albert K. Ando, *A Contribution to the Theory of Economic Fluctuations and Growth*, unpublished Ph. D. thesis, Graduate School of Industrial Administration, Carnegie Institute of Technology, May, 1959, Chapter II.

5.3. Significance of the Annual Time Paths Generated by Models II and IIE

The shortcomings of Models II and IIE in explaining the shoe, leather, hide sequence at an aggregate level result from these models being formulated in terms of behavior mechanisms intended to describe actions of typical firms. Now we must question whether these relations do in fact describe the individual behavior of firms in the shoe, leather, and hide industries. No direct test is available, since data pertaining to individual firms are lacking. An indirect test is possible, however.

Timing and distribution differences exist among the firms in a sector. Even though the mechanisms specified by our models were correct descriptions of the behavior of each individual firm, when the values of the individual firm's variables are added over all firms in a sector, there is a tendency for the high values of some firms to be offset by the low values of other firms. The resulting aggregate variables fluctuate less than the individual firm's variables. Since our models contain in effect only one firm in each sector, there can be no aggregation over firms to produce smooth sector values. However, similar results can be achieved by cumulating the monthly values for the single firm's variables over a number of months. Averaging or totaling a variable over a large number of months is a smoothing device which irons out some of the differences due to timing and distribution factors.

A partial test of whether our models describe the behavior of individual firms is to total or average the monthly values generated by the models over periods of twelve months (calendar years) and to compare these annual totals or averages with the observed annual totals or averages for the corresponding variables. A close correspondence between the annual time paths generated by our models (through totaling or averaging twelve monthly values) and the actual annual time paths would be consistent with the hypothesis that our models are formulated in terms of behavior mechanisms descriptive of large numbers of individual firms.

Charts 23 through 33 make these annual comparisons for the

eleven major endogenous variables of both models. In general, these models emerge fairly well from this comparison. Somewhat surprisingly, Model II looks a good deal better than Model IIE, especially in connection with retailers' receipts of shoes, manufacturers' shoe production, and manufacturers' receipts of leather (Charts 28, 29, and 30). The explanation for this phenomenon is that six parameters in the retailers' and manufacturers' behavioral mechanisms were estimated in such a way as to yield the best possible agreement between these relations and observed time paths *when these relations are treated as a process model rather than as a one-period-change model.*[1] Self-equilibrating features are incorporated in the behavioral mechanisms which insure that the generated time paths never depart too far from the observed paths when these relations are embedded in a process model; such features are absent from the corresponding one-period-change model.

These self-correcting features can be illustrated in connection with retailers' shoe receipts, Chart 28. Comparing this with Chart 27, the physical volume of retail shoe sales, reveals that the actual annual shoe receipts of retailers very closely mirror their actual annual sales. A similar connection, although not quite so strong, exists between retailers' annual shoe receipts and annual sales for Model II. The correspondence is completely lacking for Model IIE, where there is an inverse relation between retailers' annual receipts and sales. These considerations indicate a bias in the behavioral mechanism determining retailers' orders for shoes. When retail sales are falling, the ordering rules result in orders which are too large, and when retail sales are rising, the ordering rules result in orders which are too small.

In the process model, Model II, retailers' shoe inventories are determined by past orders generated from the model. When the ordering rules produce orders which are too large, retailers' inventories build up to an unusually high level. This high inventory level then inhibits further ordering by retailers. On the other

---

[1]These parameters are α, C_{h*}, m_l, m_u, r_l, and r_s.

hand, when their ordering rules result in orders which are too small, retailers' inventory declines to a low level. In turn, this low level of stocks stimulates the retailers to increase their orders. Thus, the process model has self-correcting features which prevent retailers' shoe receipts from getting very far out of line over any length of time.

In the one-period-change model, Model IIE, past orders generated by the model do not affect retailers' inventories. Hence, no self-equilibrating features exist to correct the bias in the retailers' ordering rules.

On the basis of Charts 23 through 33, the hypothesis that Model II is formulated in terms of behavior mechanisms which are good descriptions of some ways in which individual retailers and manufacturers operate is not refuted, even though this model does not provide a correct month-by-month description of several aggregate sector variables in the shoe, leather, hide sequence.

CHAPTER 6

Conclusions

6.1. Individual Firms and Aggregate Behavior

One of our goals in Chapter 3 was to formulate models of the shoe, leather, hide sequence which would account for the aggregate behavior of these sectors by the "typical firm" approach, i.e., by the assumption that each sector in the aggregate behaves in the same way that a representative firm belonging to this sector would behave. We proceeded in this manner to explore, to the extent possible using only aggregate data, the implications of some of the hypotheses suggested by Mrs. Mack regarding the behavior of individual firms in the retailing and manufacturing sectors. The results of Chapter 5 indicate that although Model II may include some mechanisms describing the individual behavior of large numbers of firms, our models do not provide a satisfactory explanation of the month-by-month behavior of some aggregate variables.

Satisfactory sector level models based on the "typical firm" approach may be unobtainable because individual firms in a sector operate according to quite different behavior mechanisms. Even if all firms were to have the same behavioral relations, differences in the timing of flows and the distribution of stocks among the individual firms make it unlikely that the "typical firm" approach would produce successful sector models.

In reformulating our models to seek a better understanding of the determinants of aggregate behavior in the shoe, leather, hide sequence, there are two distinct directions along which to proceed. The easier alternative is to try the traditional procedure in sector level econometric models. Micro-economic theory is used only to specify the functional dependencies among variables, and then regression techniques are used on aggregate data to estimate the forms and parameters in these functions.[1] This method may result in sector models which provide reasonably close fits between the time paths generated by these models and the observed aggregate data.[2] However, this kind of model in itself cannot shed any light upon the behavioral mechanisms which govern the operations of individual firms.

The other alternative consists in first formulating a variety of models at a micro-economic level to explain the individual behavior of specific firms in the shoe, leather, hide sequence. In order to provide a good explanation of the pricing, production, and purchasing behavior of each individual firm, it might conceivably be necessary to have as many models as there are firms, i.e., a special model for each firm. We doubt that this will be the case, however. Probably a relatively small number of basic models (perhaps something in the order of a dozen) will adequately

---

[1]An excellent example of this approach may be found in Clifford Hildreth and F. G. Jarrett, *A Statistical Study of Livestock Production and Marketing*, Cowles Commission Monograph No. 15, New York: John Wiley & Sons, 1955; London: Chapman & Hall, 1955.

[2]After this dissertation was completed, we undertook the construction of Models III and IIIE, two sector models of the shoe, leather, hide sequence which are described in Appendix A. The major difference between these new models and Models II and IIE is the use of regression equations in place of the behavioral mechanisms for the determination of retail shoe price, retailers' receipts of shoes, manufacturers' shoe production, and manufacturers' receipts of leather. The results presented in Appendix A indicate that the agreement between the generated monthly time paths of the endogenous variables and the actuals is much closer for both Models III and IIIE than for either Model II or IIE.

describe the relevant aspects of each individual firm's actions.[1] Information must be obtained regarding the number of firms in each sector which behave according to each model type. Within each model type, information is needed about the way various firms are distributed according to various parameter values. Then all these basic models of individual firms' behavior can be incorporated into an over-all computer model. This complete model can simulate the actions of each firm (or at least of a sufficiently large number of firms) and the interactions among firms which comprise the behavior of sector variables.[2] Such an approach would not involve any of the traditional "pitfalls of aggregation," for the aggregation process would consist in a straightforward summation of the values of the variables pertaining to each individual firm.[3]

The micro-economic approach to understanding sector behavior of the shoe, leather, hide sequence succeeds in avoiding the traditional "pitfalls of aggregation" only at the expense of introducing several new "problems of disaggregation," problems of allocating sales among individual firms and of obtaining precise descriptions of individual firms' behavior. Whenever any sector is analyzed into two or more groups of firms, the mechanisms by which sales are distributed among the separate groups must be specified. These relations may be of an entirely different character and considerably harder to establish than the behavioral mechanisms for individual firms.

---

[1]A good discussion of the possibility of representing superficially different kinds of entrepreneurial decision-making situations in terms of a small number of model types is found in A. Charnes and W. W. Cooper, "Management Models and Industrial Applications of Linear Programming," *Management Science*, Vol. 4, No. 1 (October, 1957), pp. 38-91.

[2]The first steps at using this approach to study the shoe, leather, hide sequence have already been undertaken as part of the Behavioral Theory of the Firm Project at the Graduate School of Industrial Administration, Carnegie Institute of Technology, where we are attempting to formulate a model describing the behavior of the shoe buyers in a large retail department store.

[3]This approach to economic model building would be hopelessly impractical without the use of electronic digital computers possessing high operating speeds and large memory capacities.

It is possible that factors which either are essentially random or else not explainable in terms of the variables included in our models become relatively more important the further one disaggregates the shoe, leather, hide sequence. Should this be the case, we might at best be able to describe the behavior of individual firms with only a low degree of reliability. If the specification errors in the models formulated for individual firms or infra-sector groups of firms cancel out on the average, then micro-economic models may yield reasonably accurate reproductions of sector behavior. Instead of canceling each other, however, these specification errors could cumulate through aggregation, leading to extremely unsatisfactory determinations of the sector variables.

If the relative distributions of some crucial variables among firms are unstable over time and if our micro-economic models succeed in reproducing these changing distributions, then the micro-economic approach might be expected to yield a more accurate determination of sector behavior than a direct aggregate approach. For example, the effects of a given aggregate level of shoe stocks in the hands of retailers on retailers' orders and sales may depend very much upon how these inventories are distributed among retailers. Should this distribution vary greatly from month to month, then aggregate relations involving retailers' shoe stocks may be fairly unreliable.

It is still a matter of conjecture which of the two methods, the traditional econometric approach dealing directly with aggregate sector variables or the micro-economic approach using models formulated in terms of variables pertaining to individual firms or infra-sector groups of firms, will ultimately result in the best sector level models.[1] There can be no doubt, however, that only the fundamental micro-economic approach can provide detailed insights concerning the processes actually used by individual firms in determining their economic behavior. Thus, in order to do more

---

[1]Our own prediction is that the second approach will provide in the long run the most successful aggregate models.

than explain the aggregate sector behavior of the shoe, leather, hide sequence and to understand the ways in which individual firms establish their selling prices and decide how much to produce and to purchase, it is necessary to formulate models which are stated entirely in terms of the behavioral mechanisms actually employed by particular firms. This will not be an easy undertaking. For such a project to succeed, it first will be necessary to obtain a considerable body of empirical information far more detailed than the kind of data with which economists usually deal, and then it will be necessary to formulate and simulate computer models far larger and more complex than any with which economists have so far worked. However, the ultimate benefit from this approach, if successful, would be enormous.

6.2. One-Period-Change Models and Process Models

In Chapter 2, we introduced the distinction between one-period-change models and process models. On a formal level, the only difference between these two kinds of models is in their treatment of lagged endogenous variables. On the interpretive level, however, these models diverge considerably concerning the assertions they make about the world.

One-period-change models state what the world will be like only one period into the future, whereas process models state what the world will be like for an arbitrarily large number of future time periods. Process models thus assert a great deal more about the nature of the world than do one-period-change models. When a body of economic theory is formulated as a precise model, the decision to regard the model as a process model or a one-period-change model should be governed by the extent to which the underlying theory is regarded as a dynamic rather than a static description of the world. With the present state of econometric methodology, however, most formal theories which really are intended to describe a dynamic process are treated as though they were one-period-change models, since the time paths generated by one-period-change models are usually thought to correspond more closely to the actual values than would be the case for process models. The results discussed in Section 5.3 indicate that we have succeeded in achieving the unexpected by producing a process model which performs better than the corresponding one-period-change model. This has been accomplished through the use of parameter estimation techniques which were specifically intended to produce a good fit when the theory is treated as a process model. The moral to be drawn is that when our econometric methodology has advanced to the point where it can cope with the special problems which arise in the treatment of theories as process models, increasing use will be made of such models in formalizing our dynamic economic theories.

6.3. Some Unsolved Methodological Problems

Four major classes of unsolved methodological problems have emerged from our work with the shoe, leather, hide models. These questions concern how functional forms should be specified, how parameters should be estimated, how process models should be validated, and how computer models should be programmed. Such issues are of fundamental importance to all attempts at using computer simulation techniques and process models.

Determining reasonable ways of specifying functional forms in computer models is necessary when the theory on which the model is based leads only to hypotheses stating that specific variables are causally determined by particular other variables, without delineating the exact form of the dependence. Our economic theories are frequently of this type. The problem has been less important in traditional econometric models, because these models most frequently are restricted to linear equations to facilitate analytic solutions. There is no reason why computer models should be similarly restricted, however, since no attempt is made to solve them analytically. Indeed, the great power of simulation techniques is their ability to handle complex, nonlinear relations. Allowing a function to be nonlinear opens up the possibility that it could have any one of a large number of possible forms. Some efficient procedures must be found for determining the proper forms of functions in these situations.

Once all the functional forms in a model are specified, several parameters which have not been assigned numerical values usually remain. This assignment must be made before the model can be simulated. The values of the parameters should be estimated to secure the best fit between the model and the world it is intended to describe. A process model is intended to describe evolutionary behavior over many successive time periods. Furthermore, a process model involves a very high order of joint determination of all the endogenous variables, stretching over the entire time span which is simulated. Relatively recent advances in econometric methodology indicate that unbiased and efficient parameter estimates can be obtained only when explicit account is taken of the simultaneous character of the equations in the model. Should these results carry over into process models, obtaining maximum likelihood estimates of all the parameters in such models would be an extremely formidable task.

A more feasible approach to the parameter estimation problem may be to restrict attention to the joint determination of only the current endogenous variables within a single period and to consider that the values of the lagged endogenous variables are subject to errors. The parameter estimation problem must then be considered within the framework of an "errors in the variables" model rather than an "errors in the equations" model. A few econometricians have investigated this kind of estimation problem, and their results may be applicable with little modification to computer models.[1]

The likelihood of a process model incorrectly describing the world is very high, because it makes some strong assertions about

---

[1]Recent surveys of the state of econometric methodology regarding errors in the variables models can be found in J. D. Sargan, "The Estimation of Economic Relationships Using Instrumental Variables," *Econometrica*, Vol. 26, No. 3 (July, 1958), pp. 393-415; and in Albert Madansky, "The Fitting of Straight Lines When Both Variables Are Subject to Error," *Journal of the American Statistical Association*, Vol. 54, No. 285 (March, 1959), pp. 173-205.

the nature of the world. However, there are various degrees by which any model can fail to describe the world, so it is meaningful to say that some models are more adequate descriptions of the world than are others. Some criteria must be devised to indicate when the time paths generated by a process model agree sufficiently with the observed time paths so that the agreement cannot be attributed to mere coincidence. Tests must be devised for the "goodness of fit" of process models with the real world. The problem of model validation becomes even more difficult if available data about the "actual" behavior of the world are themselves subject to error.[1]

The final problem in connection with further work with computer models is the need for developing more suitable programming languages. The ability to work flexibly and rapidly with computer models is currently hampered by the state of the programming art. Once a computer model has been fully specified in flow-chart form, the task of programming and running the model should be almost automatic. Some of the various scientific compilers now available are reasonably suitable, but they can be considerably improved to facilitate work with computer models. The following additional features would be desirable:

1. The ability to use symbolic names for the variables which are identical with the symbols used originally in formulating the model;
2. The ability to manipulate symbols and numbers with equal facility;

_____

[1]In private conversation, Professor Jack Johnston, currently of the University of Manchester, has suggested three different ways of approaching the validation problem for process models: (a) using distribution-free statistical methods to test whether the actual and generated series display similar timing and amplitude characteristics; (b) running a simple regression of the generated series as a function of the actual series and testing whether the resulting regression equation has an intercept which is not significantly different from zero and a slope which is not significantly different from unity; (c) running a factor analysis on the set of generated time paths and a second factor analysis on the set of observed time paths, and testing whether the two groups of factor loadings are significantly different from each other. We have not yet attempted to apply any of these tests or to work out the formal details which they would involve.

3. The ability to make any part of the model, no matter how small, a closed subroutine, to allow local changes in the model to be made quickly and easily;

4. The ability to perform automatically the necessary housekeeping for segmenting the program and allocating all storage locations, including the use of auxiliary storage when necessary;

5. The automatic ability to handle a wide variety of input and output formats, including the reading and plotting of graphs.

6.4. Potential Applications of the Shoe, Leather, Hide Models

A computer model which can provide an accurate description of the aggregative behavior of shoe retailers, shoe manufacturers, and cattlehide leather tanners, will have a number of uses both on a practical and on a theoretical plane.

The business firms which comprise the shoe, leather, hide sequence can use the model (presuming that it describes the current structure of the market) to predict the relevant future behavior of the environment in which they are immersed. If these predictions are accurate, then this information would be extremely helpful to the firms in their own decision-making processes. An aggregate sector model cannot per se automatically provide an individual firm with optimal decisions, but it can provide those forecasts of the relevant environmental behavior which are needed for optimal decision-making and planning.[1]

The government can use the model (again presuming that it describes the current structure of the market) to predict the consequences with respect to the shoe, leather, and hide industries

---

[1]A fundamental micro-economic model of the shoe, leather, hide sequence which adquately describes not only the aggregate variables but also the individual behavior of firms in these industries would be of much greater practical importance. In the process of formulating such a model, a great deal of information must be developed concerning the decision rules used by particular firms. Once these relations are formalized, an operations research study could easily be made to improve the decision-making processes of these individual firms.

of various kinds of governmental actions, and hence to help determine the desirability of such actions. The kinds of governmental behavior which can be analyzed with such a computer model include the imposition of a sales tax on shoes, changes in disposable personal income through general tax changes, procurement of large quantities of shoes for the military services, and changes in the tariffs on imported hides. Such changes can be readily incorporated in the structure of the model, and we can then simulate the resulting model to determine the effects of the changes on prices, sales, production, and orders throughout the entire shoe, leather, hide sequence.

On the theoretical level, there are several interesting investigations of a shoe, leather, hide process model to be made. The dynamic properties of the model can be examined to determine the long-run equilibrium tendencies of the model, the stability of the model when displaced from equilibrium, and the dynamic responses of the system to such artificial types of forcing functions (for the exogenous variables) as pulse functions, step functions, ramp functions, and sine functions.

Finally, our aggregate model of the shoe, leather, hide sequence can be embedded into other computer models. By combining similar models for various segments of the economy, a complex but realistic computer model for the entire economy can be developed.

Just as several computer models can be combined into one over-all model, any complex computer model can be divided into several component submodels. An analysis of separate portions of a computer model may be both a practical necessity and a theoretical aid.

Techniques for estimating parameters in a process model should consider the joint determination of variables by the system both within and between time periods. One procedure for this is to simulate the model using different sets of values for the parameters in order to determine those values which result in the best fit between the time paths generated by the model and those actually observed. If the model is at all large and the time periods over which it extends are at all numerous, it may be impractical to run the model for very many sets of parameter values. A way around this difficulty lies in simulating only a small subsystem of the model for parameter estimation purposes.

The values of α and C_{h*} in the retailers' shoe ordering rules and the values of r_s, r_l, m_l, and m_u in the manufacturers' leather purchasing rules were estimated for Model II by this procedure.[1]

A complex process model may explain some of its variables better than others. A good way of discovering this is to simulate various component submodels separately. Departures of the generated time paths from the actuals within a subsystem are then clearly traceable to specification errors within that portion of the model. It must be emphasized that the dissection of the over-all model into component parts serves only as a diagnostic tool. Our goal must remain that of obtaining an explanation of the behavior of the entire system.

To illustrate the kinds of diagnostic insights that subsectioning a process model can provide, portions of Model II were run as process submodels. Equations (4) through (6), (9) through (29), (31), and (32) are a submodel which determines retailers' selling price, orders, and receipts and manufacturers' production; this is called the "retailers' process model subsystem." Retail shoe sales, factory shoe price, and average hide price are the endogenous variables of Model II which are exogenous variables in the retailers' process model subsystem. Simulating this submodel can show the immediate effect of the behavioral mechanisms adopted for retailers' shoe orders without these being clouded by specification errors elsewhere in the system. Charts 34, 35, and 36 show

---

[1]It should be realized that estimating parameter values from subsystems is only a heuristic procedure, which in principle may occasionally produce difficulties. Even if all parameter values were estimated in a way which produced close correspondence between the time paths generated by each submodel and the actual values, when the subsystems are embedded into a single over-all model unforeseen interactions between the component parts may occur. The final test of the goodness of fit of a process model must deal with the model as a whole rather than with its parts in isolation.

the time paths generated by the retailers' process model subsystem for retail shoe price, retailers' shoe receipts, and manufacturers' shoe production. Comparing Chart 35 with Chart 11 reveals that most of the extreme fluctuations in retailers' shoe receipts generated by Model II arise from the form of the retailers' ordering rules rather than from elsewhere in the system.

The "manufacturers' process model subsystem" was defined as equations (38) through (45); this portion of Model II determines manufacturers' leather receipts. Factory shoe price, leather price, average hide price, and manufacturers' shoe production play the role of exogenous variables in this submodel, although they are endogenous in Model II as a whole. Chart 37 pictures the time path traced by manufacturers' leather receipts in the manufacturers' process model subsystem. Comparing Chart 37 with Chart 15 reveals that most of the bad performance of the generated leather receipts series in Model II stemmed not from the behavioral mechanism determining manufacturers' purchases but from other parts of the model.[1]

6.5. Advantages of Computer Models

Chapter 1 stated our twofold purpose in this thesis to extend our understanding of behavior in the shoe, leather, and hide industries and to investigate the usefulness of computer models and simulation techniques in economics. Having reached the end of our journey, we shall summarize our observations concerning the latter issue.

The main advantage of using computer simulation as a tool in economics is to provide a concrete procedure for formulating and testing hypotheses. A frequent objection raised against mathematical models of economic systems is that the models are unrealistic. This is often true, usually because adding realism

---

[1] In Model II, retailers' orders for shoes act as a violent forcing function on manufacturers' shoe production, which in turn imparts severe fluctuations to manufacturers' leather purchases.

requires adding complexity as well. Since most mathematical models are intended for analytical solution, their complexity and realism must be severely limited. Computer models, however, can be made as complex and realistic as our theories permit, for analytical solutions to these models are unnecessary. No matter how complicated the formulation of the model, simulation techniques enable us to trace out the consequences of the model. Hence, economic theories can be cast into a precise model without distortion of the meaning embodied in the theories, and the descriptions of the world implied by these theories can be determined.

The formulation of economic theories in terms of computer models provides opportunities for working with formal models to nonmathematical economists. People need not be powerful mathematicians in order to build and run computer models. It requires a much more extensive knowledge of mathematics to obtain an analytical solution to a complex mathematical model than it does to formulate the model. When simulation techniques are used, however, once the model is set up, the rest is relatively easy.

A further advantage of computer models is the ease of modifying the assumptions of the model. When suitable programming languages become available, equations can be inserted, deleted, or changed in the model, and only local changes which can be quickly made will be required in the program. Modifications of this kind will have a much smaller effect on the ease with which the model can be simulated than they would on the difficulty of obtaining analytical solutions.

The use of computer process models can provide much greater insights into the dynamic implications of economic theories. Understanding the nature of the behavior through time of the economic forces may become synonymous with being able to program and simulate these forces.

The use of computer simulation techniques seems especially well adapted to the development of behavioral models at a micro-economic level. Trying to formulate a detailed computer model of the actions of individual households or firms spotlights the kind of empirical information needed to obtain a better understanding of these activities. It is only when all the detailed aspects of entrepreneurial decision-making can be programmed and simulated successfully that we will have a behavioral theory of the firm, "a theory that takes the firm as its unit of study and the prediction of firm behavior with respect to such decisions as price, output, resource allocation, etc. as its objective."[1]

---

[1]R. M. Cyert and James G. March, "Introduction to Research on a Behavioral Theory of the Firm," Behavioral Theory of the Firm Project Working Paper No. 1, Graduate School of Industrial Administration, Carnegie Institute of Technology, Oct. 17, 1957, p. 2.

MODELS III AND IIIE[1]

We have seen in Chapter 5 that Models II and IIE fail to provide adequate explanations of the monthly behavior of several aggregate variables, even though there is some evidence that Model II may include some mechanisms describing the individual behavior of large numbers of firms. As we pointed out in Section 6.1, one possible way of restructuring our models to produce a more satisfactory determination of aggregate behavior in the shoe, leather, hide sequence is the traditional procedure in sector level econometric models. This approach has been carried out in Models III and IIIE, a process model and a one-period-change model, respectively.

In Models II and IIE, all of the major endogenous variables are determined by regression equations except for retail shoe price, retailers' receipts of shoes, manufacturers' production of shoes, and manufacturers' receipts of leather; behavioral mechanisms are used for the determination of these variables. Models III and IIIE are the same as Models II and IIE except that the behavioral relations found in Models II and IIE are replaced, in Models III and IIIE, by regression equations. The factors considered for inclusion as independent variables in these regression equations were all suggested by the behavioral mechanisms which they replace.

The retailers' selling price for shoes in Models II and IIE is determined by equations (5) and (6). In Models III and IIIE, these two equations are replaced by the following regression equation:

$$(63) \quad Rp(t) = C_{0,63} + C_{1,63}Rp(t-1) + C_{2,63}Fp(t) + C_{3,63}Fp(t-2)$$

All the regression coefficients in equation (63) are statistically significant at the 5 per cent level or better. The single equation least squares estimates of these coefficients and (in parentheses) the number of times each estimate exceeds its standard error are:

---

[1]Appendix A was added after this dissertation was accepted in partial fulfillment of the requirements for the Ph.D. degree at Carnegie Institute of Technology.

$C_{0,63} = .0620$

$C_{1,63} = .845 \ (21.1)$

$C_{2,63} = .495 \ (8.8)$

$C_{3,63} = -.271 \ (3.8)$

The multiple correlation coefficient adjusted for degrees of freedom is .997.

The behavioral mechanism by which retailers' receipts of shoes are determined in Models II and IIE consists of equations (8) through (29). In Models III and IIIE, all these relations are replaced by the following regression equation:

$$(64) \quad \Sigma(t) = C_{0,64} + C_{1,64}[S(t-1) + S(t-2) + S(t-3)] \times [S(t-4)$$
$$+ S(t-5) + S(t-6) + S(t-7) + S(t-8) + S(t-9)]$$
$$\div [S(t-13) + S(t-14) + S(t-15)] + C_{2,64}[Hp(t-1)$$
$$- Hp(t-4)] \div Hp(t-4) + C_{3,64}M_\Sigma(t)$$

The regression coefficients in equation (64) are all statistically significant at the 5 per cent level or better. Single equation least squares techniques produced the following estimates of the regression coefficients (shown in parentheses is the number of times each coefficient exceeds its standard error):

$C_{0,64} = -20,200,000$

$C_{1,64} = .124 \ (9.5)$

$C_{2,64} = 4,610,000 \ (2.5)$

$C_{3,64} = 281,000 \ (6.8)$

The multiple coefficient of correlation adjusted for degrees of freedom is .74.

Manufacturers' shoe production is specified by equation (32) in Models II and IIE. This mechanism is replaced in Models III and IIIE by the following regression relation:

$$(65) \quad P(t) = C_{0,65} + C_{1,65}P(t-1) + C_{2,65}\Sigma(t)$$
$$+ C_{3,65}\Sigma(t-4) + C_{4,65}G^S(t-1) + C_{5,65}M_P(t)$$

In equation (65), all the coefficients are statistically significant at the 5 per cent level or better. Using single equation least squares estimation techniques, the following estimates of the regression coefficients and (in parentheses) the number of times each coefficient exceeds its standard error were obtained:

$$C_{0,65} = -13,000,000$$
$$C_{1,65} = .334 \ (5.8)$$
$$C_{2,65} = .261 \ (4.5)$$
$$C_{3,65} = .154 \ (3.6)$$
$$C_{4,65} = -.0366 \ (2.8)$$
$$C_{5,65} = 219,000 \ (8.9)$$

The multiple correlation coefficient, adjusted for degrees of freedom, is .88.

In Models II and IIE, the leather purchases by manufacturers are determined by the complex mechanism defined in equations (34) through (45). These relations are all replaced in Models III and IIIE by the following regression equation:

$$(66) \qquad L(t) = C_{0,66} + C_{1,66}L(t-1) + C_{2,66}[P(t) - P(t-12)]$$
$$+ C_{3,66}\frac{P(t)}{G(t-1)} + C_{4,66}M_L(t)$$

Single equation least squares estimation yielded the following estimates for the regression coefficients and (in parentheses) the number of times each coefficient exceeds its standard error:

$$C_{0,66} = -1,210,000$$
$$C_{1,66} = .694 \ (13.2)$$
$$C_{2,66} = .0118 \ (4.1)$$
$$C_{3,66} = 4,370 \ (3.5)$$
$$C_{4,66} = 16,300 \ (3.3)$$

The coefficient of multiple correlation adjusted for degrees of freedom is .87.

Models III and IIIE are both defined by the same set of equations. They differ from each other only in that Model III is a process model, whereas Model IIIE is a one-period-change model. [1]

---

[1]Model IIIE is a true one-period-change model, because *all* lagged endogenous variables appearing in Model IIIE are replaced by their observed values. In contrast, Model IIE was not quite a true one-period-change model, because the lack of actual data on retailers' orders for shoes from 1930 through 1940 made it necessary to use the generated rather than the actual values for retailers' shoe orders whenever these appeared as lagged variables in Model IIE. This problem does not arise in Model IIIE, however, since retailers' orders for shoes play no explicit role in this model.

Models III and IIIE were programmed for and simulated on Carnegie Institute of Technology's IBM 650 RAMAC electronic digital computer. The actual programs are straightforward modifications, made at the compiler level, of the programs for Models II and IIE described in Chapter 4. Since the forms of several functions are simpler in Models III and IIIE than in Models II and IIE, the running times required in simulating each month for Models III and IIIE are only forty seconds and fifty-five seconds, respectively, in contrast to sixty seconds and seventy-five seconds required for Models II and IIE, respectively.

The monthly time paths for 1930 through 1940 generated by the simulation runs for both Models III and IIIE are in much closer agreement to the observed time paths than was the case for Models II and IIE. Charts 38 through 59 compare the values generated by our models for the eleven major endogenous variables with the actual values. For no variable does Model III produce a better fit than does Model IIIE[1], a result which was to be expected since all parameters in these models were estimated using single equation least squares techniques.[2]

On the basis of these visual comparisons, Models III and IIIE seem to succeed extremely well in reproducing the monthly behavior of the major sector variables in the shoe, leather, hide sequence. On the whole, Model III does a reasonably satisfactory job of following the major swings in the time paths of the actual series, a fairly impressive accomplishment in view of the large numbers of degrees of freedom which are present. However, a more refined analysis of the degree to which Model III describes aggregate behavior in the shoe, leather, and hide industries must await the development of "goodness of fit" tests for process models, a problem discussed in Section 6.3. Although it would be possible within the framework of currently available econometric methodology to subject Model IIIE to more refined "goodness of fit" tests, this does not seem worthwhile in view of the fact that our available data on the "actual" behavior of several important sector variables is itself suspect.

---

[1]The upward bias in the time path for manufacturers' shoe production generated by Model IIIE in 1940 (see Chart 51) arises from a fundamental defect in the "actual" series for manufacturers' finished shoe stocks. The only available data for these inventories show them suddenly dropping to an obviously too low level early in 1940, even being negative in some months. In Model IIIE, manufacturers' shoe production depends upon the "actual" manufacturers' finished shoe stocks, but in Model III, it depends instead on the generated manufacturers' finished inventories. Hence, Model III produces a better fit in 1940 for manufacturers' shoe production than does Model IIIE (compare Charts 50 and 51).

[2]The assumptions on which least squares estimation procedures rest are more nearly satisfied by one-period-change models than by process models.

A thorough revision of many of the time series used as representations of actual behavior in the shoe, leather, and hide industries would be desirable before undertaking any further reformulations of our models. Our only purpose in presenting Models III and IIIE is to demonstrate that computer models of the shoe, leather, hide sequence can be devised which do a much more adequate job of reproducing observed monthly sector level behavior than do Models II and IIE.

OBTAINING ACTUAL DATA ON THE SHOE, LEATHER, HIDE SEQUENCE

In May, 1958, Mrs. Mack very generously allowed us to copy a considerable amount of data from her files at the National Bureau of Economic Research. Thus, we generally had access to all of the time series used by Mrs. Mack in her study of the shoe, leather, hide sequence.[1]

Several data collection problems still remained, however. A few of the time series which Mrs. Mack used were not readily locatable in her files. Furthermore, for the purpose of studying the propagation and transmission of cyclical and subcyclical fluctuations through the various vertical stages of the shoe, leather, hide sequence, it was necessary for Mrs. Mack to deal exclusively with seasonally adjusted series. Our models, however, are formulated in terms of current monthly values, not seasonally adjusted monthly values. It was therefore necessary to supplement Mrs. Mack's series with data from other sources, and to process substantial numbers of time series to remove the effects of seasonal adjustments which had been made in them. In some cases, the procedures used in obtaining the "actual" data were *ad hoc* methods which may well have introduced spurious noise in a few of the series. At a later date, a thorough revision of our actual data on the shoe, leather, hide sequence might be desirable.

We now indicate the methods by which we obtained actual data for all the major *ex post* variables of our models with the exception of retailers' orders for shoes. In this description, RPM(n) denotes data obtained from Mrs. Mack's files corresponding to series number (n) in her book.[2]

$Bls(t)$ BLS consumers' price index in month t, 1935–39 = 100. Source: RPM(124).

---

[1] A list and description of these series and their sources is found in Mack, *op. cit.*, pp. 263-283.

[2] *Ibid.*

$Dpi(t)$ Disposable personal income in month t, \$.
Source: *Survey of Current Business*, "Total Income Payments," raw data. These monthly values were adjusted to agree with the annual totals for "Former Concept, Statistically Revised," *National Income*, 1947, p. 14.

$Fp(t)$ Factory shoe price (manufacturers' selling price of shoes) in month t, \$/pair.
Source: Seasonally adjusted RPM(41) divided by seasonally adjusted RPM(39), since RPM(2) was unavailable.

$G(t)$ Manufacturers' leather stocks at end of month t, equivalent hides.
Source: Analogous to the derivation of RPM(75), but using raw data instead of seasonally adjusted series.

$G^S(t)$ Manufacturers' finished shoe stocks at end of month t, pairs.
Source: $H(t) + G^S(t)$ was obtained analogously to the derivation of RPM(48), but using raw data instead of seasonally adjusted series. We then obtained $H(t)$ from seasonally adjusted RPM(54) and seasonally adjusted RPM(48) by assuming that $H(t)$ and $H(t) + G^S(t)$ have the same seasonal pattern. $G^S(t)$ was then found by subtracting $H(t)$ from $H(t) + G^S(t)$.

$H(t)$ Retailers' shoe stocks at end of month t, pairs.
Source: See discussion of $G^S(t)$.

$Hp(t)$ Average price of hides in month t, \$/equivalent hide.
Source: *Survey of Current Business*, "Index Numbers of Wholesale Prices, Hides and Skins, 1926 = 100," converted to \$/equivalent hide.

$Hp^C(t)$ Country hide price in month t, \$/pound.
Source: Through 1933 from *Wholesale Prices*, Bureau of Labor Statistics. From 1934 on, assuming the seasonal index of the ratio of country hide price to packer hide price from 1922–1933 applies after 1933, raw data on country hide prices was computed from RPM(26), $Hp^P(t)$, and $Hp^I(t)$.

$Hp^I(t)$ Imported hide price in month t, \$/pound.
Source: $Hp^P(t)$ divided by RPM(24).

$Hp^P(t)$ Packer hide price in month t, \$/pound.
Source: *Commodity Year Book*.

$Hp^R(t)$ Hide price ratio in month t, pure number.
Source: The mean of $Hp^C(t)$ and $Hp^I(t)$, divided by $Hp^P(t)$.

$J^H(t)$ Tanners' stocks of hides at end of month t, equivalent hides.
Source: RPM(98).

$J^I(t)$ Tanners' stocks of in-process leather at end of month t, equivalent hides.
Source: *Commodity Yearbook.*

$J^L(t)$ Tanners' stocks of finished leather at end of month t, equivalent hides.
Source: RPM(114) minus RPM(112).

$L(t)$ Manufacturers' leather purchases in month t, equivalent hides.
Source: RPM(89) and *Commodity Yearbook.*

$Lp(t)$ Leather price in month t, \$/equivalent hide.
Source: *Survey of Current Business*, "Index Numbers of Wholesale Prices, Leather, 1926 = 100," converted to \$/equivalent hide.

$P(t)$ Shoe production in month t, pairs.
Source: RPM(40).

$Q(t)$ Tanners' orders for all hides in month t, equivalent hides.
Source: RPM(104).

$Q^C(t)$ Tanners' orders for country hides in month t, equivalent hides.
Source: Equivalent to $R^C(t)$.

$Q^I(t)$ Tanners' orders for imported hides in month t, equivalent hides.
Source: Equivalent to $R^I(t + 2)$.

$Q^P(t)$ Tanners' orders for packer hides in month t, equivalent hides.
Source: Equivalent to $R^P(t)$.

$R(t)$ Tanners' receipts of all hides in month t, equivalent hides.
Source: RPM(103).

$R^C(t)$ Tanners' receipts of country hides in month t, equivalent hides.
Source: RPM(107) and seasonally adjusted RPM(103), assuming the seasonal index of $R^C(t)$ is the same as the seasonal index of $R(t)$.

$R^D(t)$ Tanners' receipts of domestic hides in month t, equivalent hides.
Source: The sum of $R^P(t)$ and $R^C(t)$.

$R^I(t)$ Tanners' receipts of imported hides in month t, equivalent hides.
Source: RPM(105).

$R^P(t)$ Tanners' receipts of packer hides in month t, equivalent hides.
Source: RPM(108) and seasonally adjusted RPM(103), assuming the seasonal index of $R^C(t)$ is the same as the seasonal index of $R(t)$.

$Rp(t)$ Retail price of shoes in month t, \$/pair.
Source: Seasonally adjusted RPM(31) divided by seasonally adjusted RPM(33), since RPM(9) was unavailable.

$S(t)$ Retailers' shoe sales in month t, pairs.
Source: $[SRp](t)$ divided by $Rp(t)$.

$[SRp](t)$ Retailers' shoe sales in month t, \$.
Source: Seasonally adjusted RPM(31), corrected by some average seasonal indexes to remove the adjustments made for the month of the year, the date of Easter, and the number of Saturdays and Sundays in the month.[1]

$W(t)$ Tanners' hide wettings (hides entering the leather production process) in month t, equivalent hides.
Source: RPM(68).

$X(t)$ Finished leather production in month t, equivalent hides.
Source: RPM(64).

$\Gamma(t)$ Hide stocks in the hands of packers, butchers, and hide dealers at the end of month t, equivalent hides.
Source: RPM(99).

$\Sigma(t)$ Retailers' receipts of shoes in month t, pairs.
Source: $S(t)$ plus $H(t)$ minus $H(t-1)$.

---

[1]The indexes used are found in Ruth P. Mack, *Factors Influencing Consumption: An Experimental Analysis of Shoe Buying*, Technical Paper 10, New York: National Bureau of Economic Research, 1954, pp. 81-82, 89n, 91, and 91n.

CHARTS

Chart 1

RETAIL SHOE PRICE

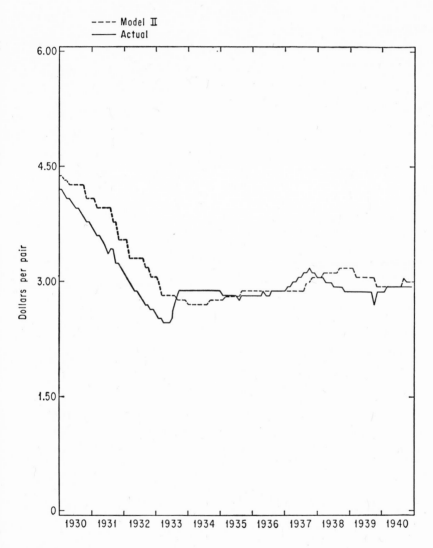

---- Model II
—— Actual

Chart 2

RETAIL SHOE PRICE

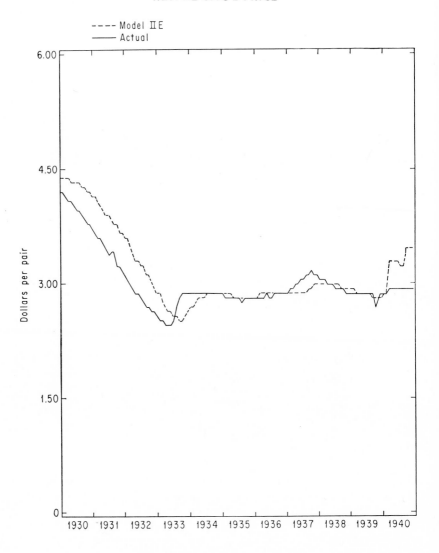

96

Chart 3

FACTORY SHOE PRICE

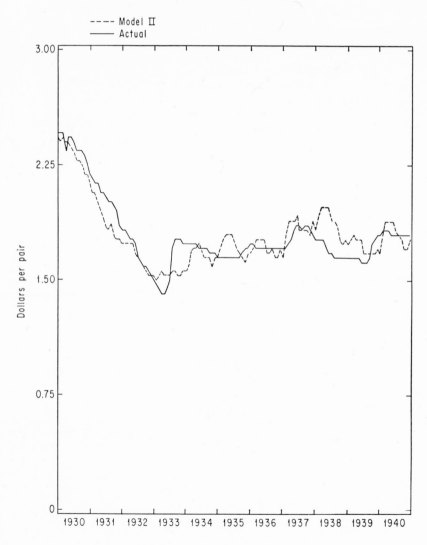

Chart 4

FACTORY SHOE PRICE

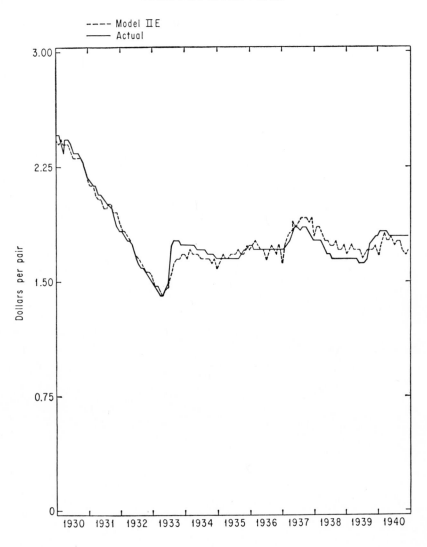

Chart 5

LEATHER PRICE

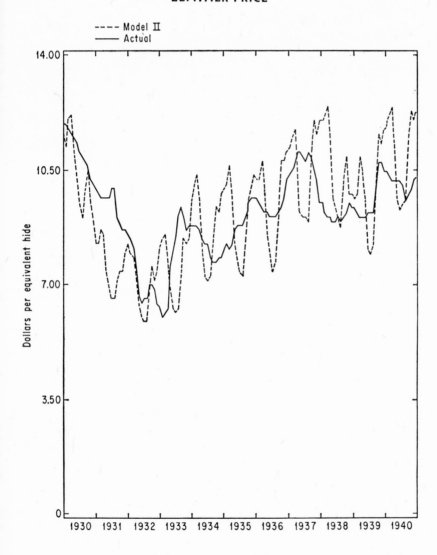

---- Model II
——— Actual

14.00

10.50

Dollars per equivalent hide

7.00

3.50

0

1930 1931 1932 1933 1934 1935 1936 1937 1938 1939 1940

99

Chart 6

LEATHER PRICE

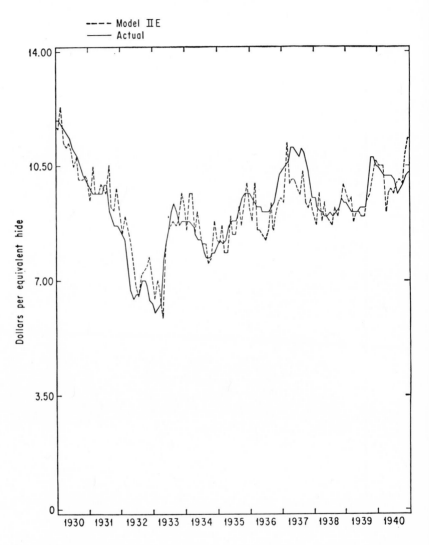

Chart 7

AVERAGE HIDE PRICE

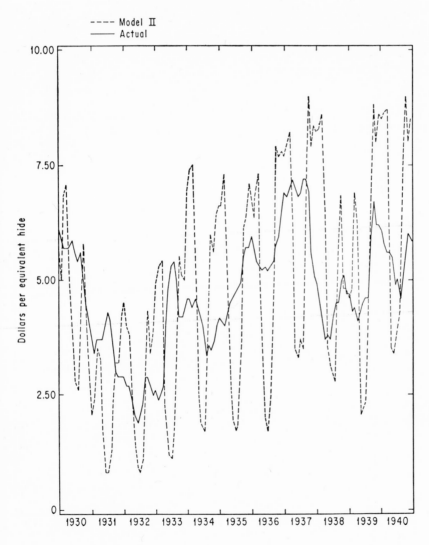

- - - - Model II
——— Actual

Dollars per equivalent hide

10.00

7.50

5.00

2.50

0

1930 1931 1932 1933 1934 1935 1936 1937 1938 1939 1940

Chart 8

AVERAGE HIDE PRICE

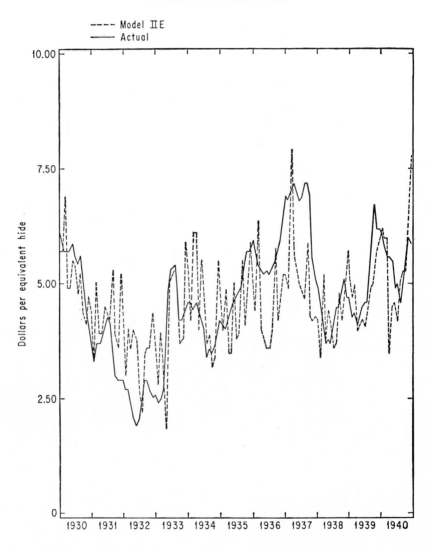

Chart 9

RETAIL SHOE SALES, PAIRS

---- Model II
—— Actual

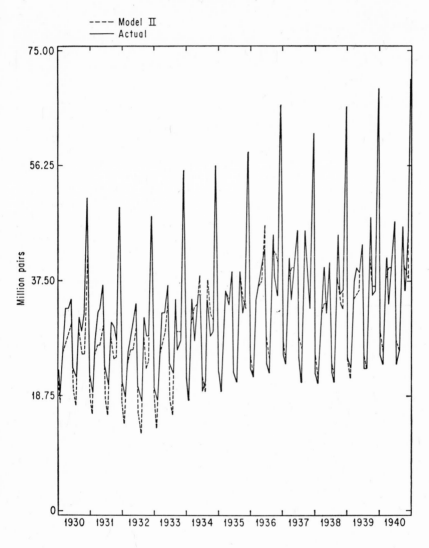

Chart 10

RETAIL SHOE SALES, PAIRS

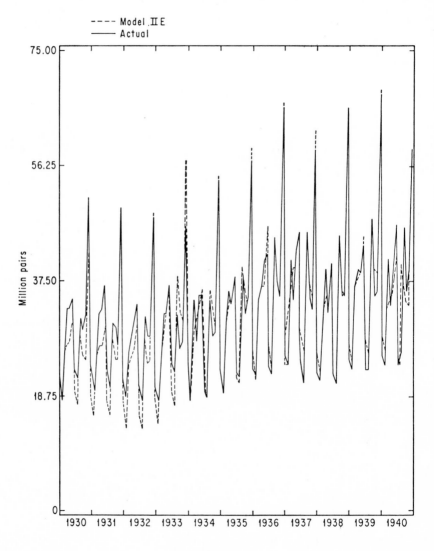

---- Model II E
—— Actual

Chart 11

RETAILERS' RECEIPTS OF SHOES

----- Model II
——— Actual

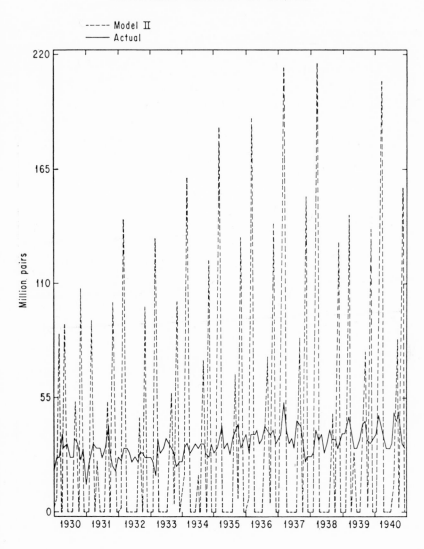

Chart 12

RETAILERS' RECEIPTS OF SHOES

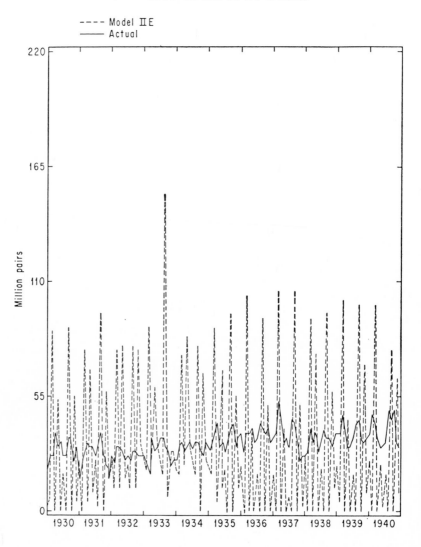

---- Model II E
—— Actual

Chart 13

MANUFACTURERS' SHOE PRODUCTION

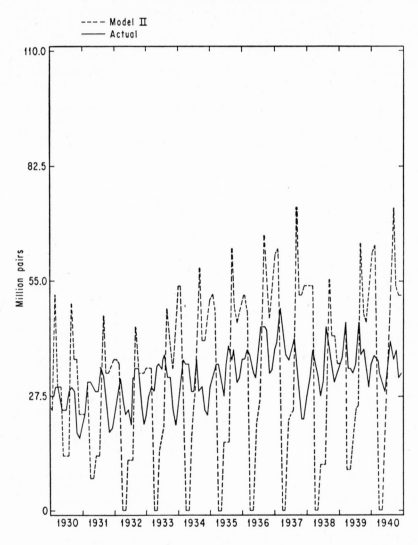

---- Model II
—— Actual

Chart 14

MANUFACTURERS' SHOE PRODUCTION

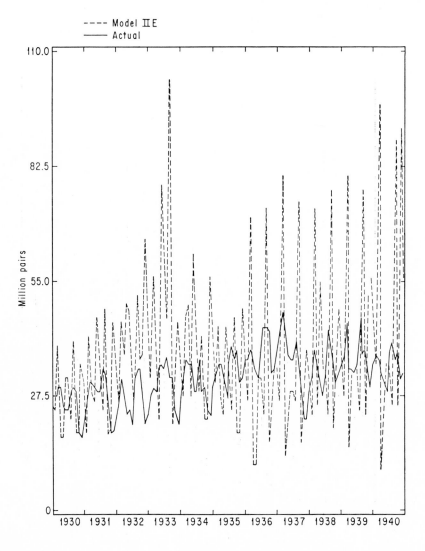

---- Model II E
—— Actual

Chart 15

MANUFACTURERS' RECEIPTS OF LEATHER

----- Model II
—— Actual

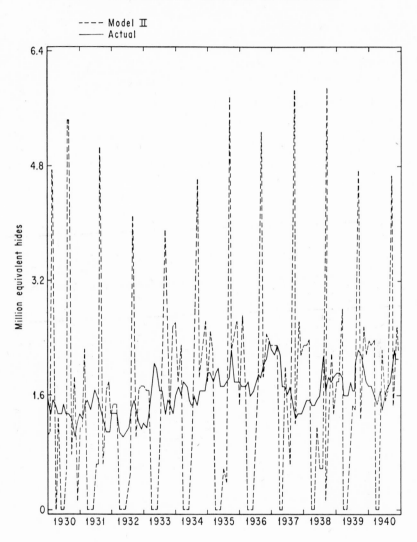

109

Chart 16

MANUFACTURERS' RECEIPTS OF LEATHER

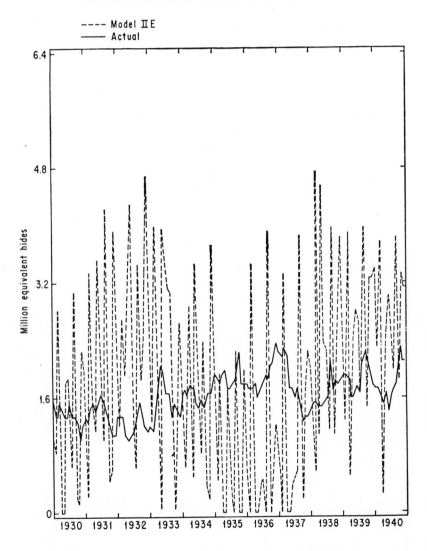

Chart 17

TANNERS' FINISHED LEATHER PRODUCTION

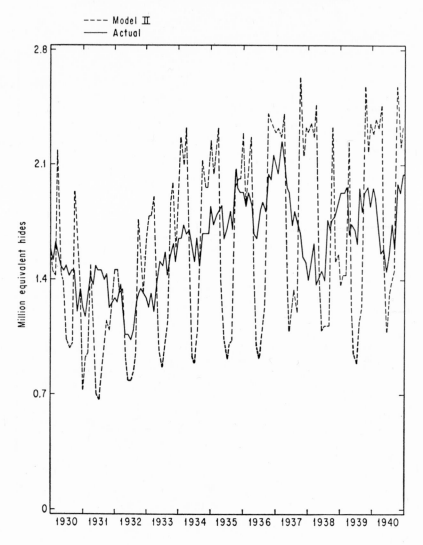

Chart 18

TANNERS' FINISHED LEATHER PRODUCTION

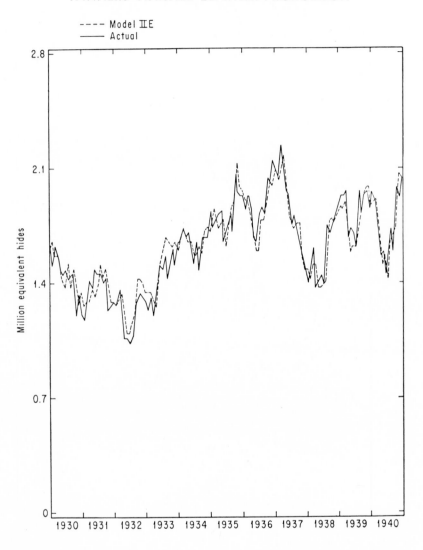

---- Model $\mathrm{I\!I}$E
——— Actual

Chart 19

TANNERS' HIDE WETTINGS

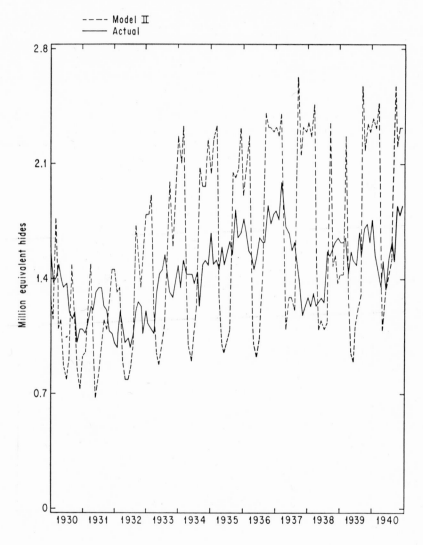

113

Chart 20

TANNERS' HIDE WETTINGS

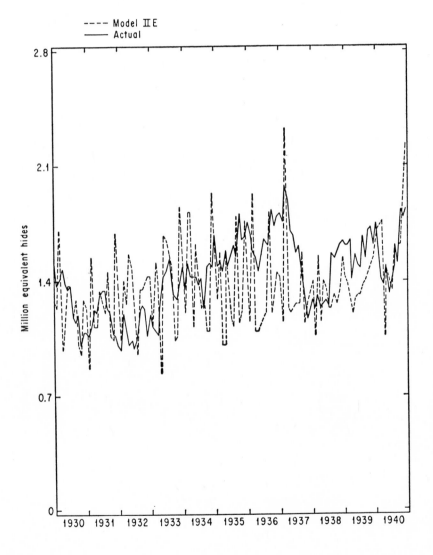

---- Model II E
—— Actual

Chart 21

TANNERS' RECEIPTS OF ALL HIDES

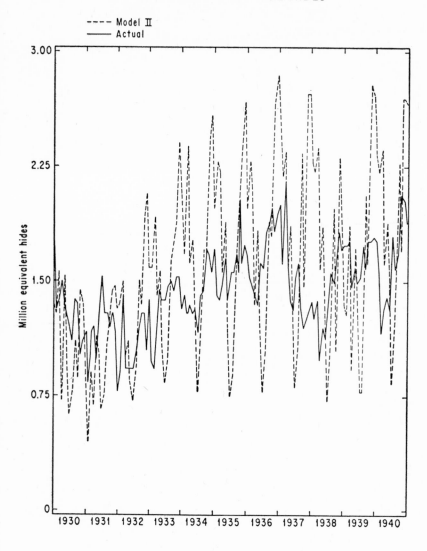

---- Model II
—— Actual

115

Chart 22

TANNERS' RECEIPTS OF ALL HIDES

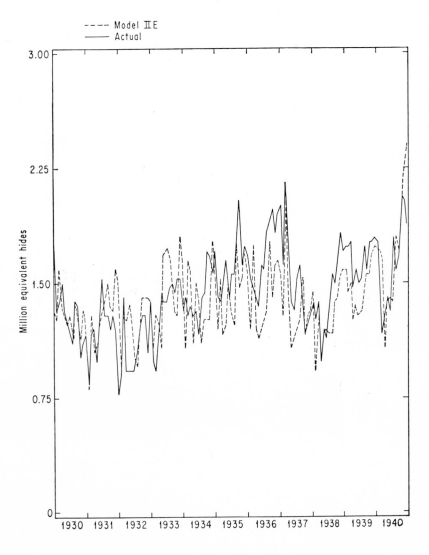

---- Model II E
——— Actual

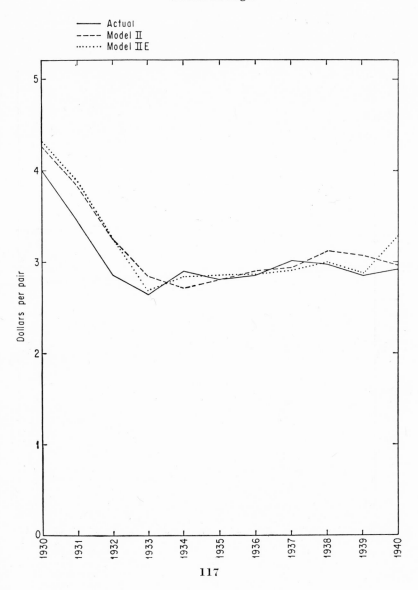

Chart 23

RETAIL SHOE PRICE

Annual Averages

——— Actual
– – – Model II
········ Model II E

Dollars per pair

117

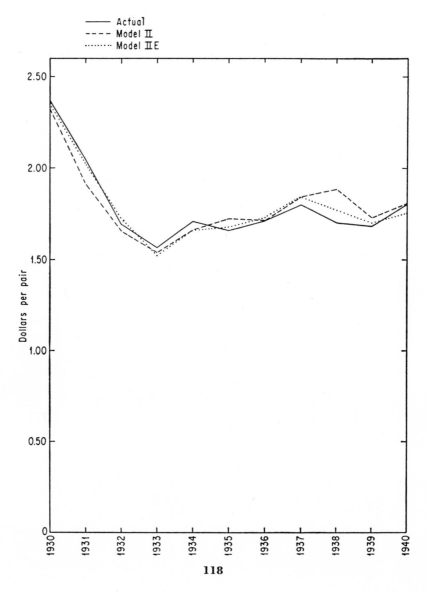

Chart 24

FACTORY SHOE PRICE

Annual Averages

——— Actual
- - - Model II
·········· Model II E

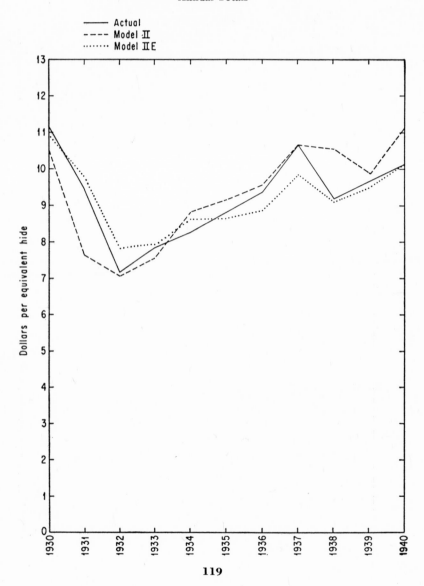

Chart 25

LEATHER PRICES

Annual Totals

——— Actual
– – – Model II
·········· Model II E

Chart 26

AVERAGE HIDE PRICES

Annual Totals

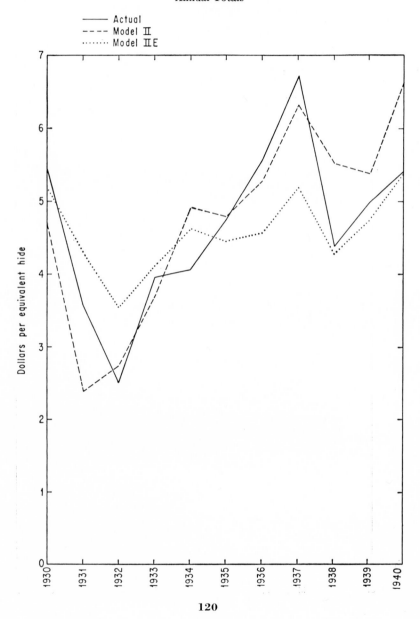

Chart 27

RETAIL SHOE SALES, PAIRS

Annual Totals

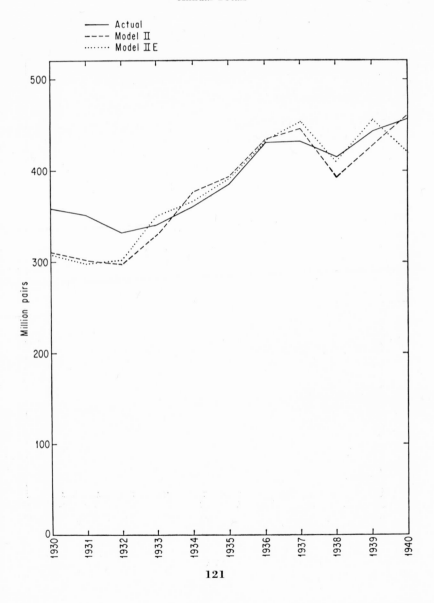

Chart 28

RETAILERS' SHOE RECEIPTS

Annual Totals

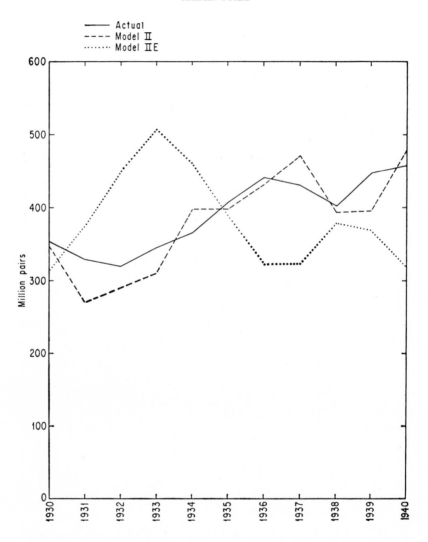

Chart 29

MANUFACTURERS' SHOE PRODUCTION

Annual Totals

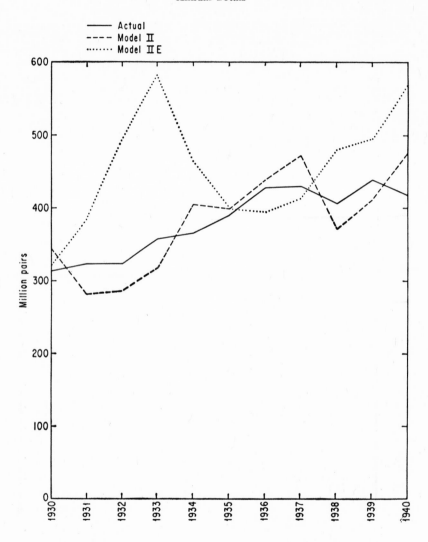

Chart 30

MANUFACTURERS' LEATHER RECEIPTS

Annual Totals

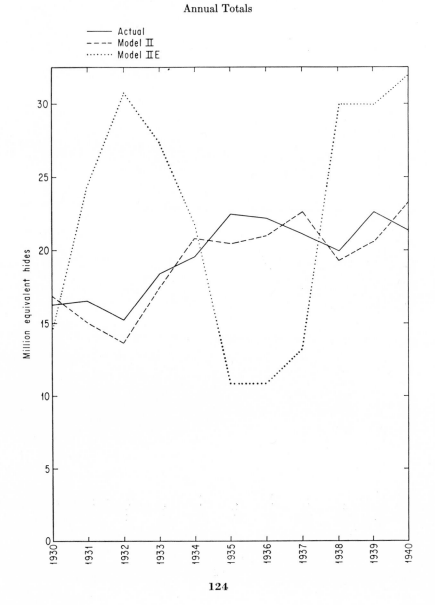

Chart 31

TANNERS' FINISHED LEATHER PRODUCTION
Annual Totals

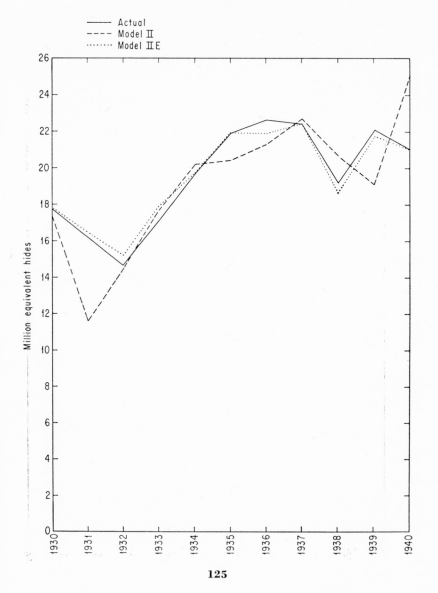

Actual
Model II
Model II E

Million equivalent hides

Chart 32

HIDE WETTINGS

Annual Totals

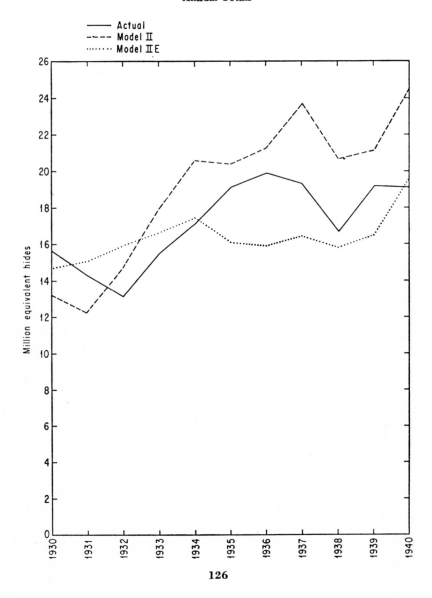

Chart 33

TANNERS' RECEIPTS OF ALL HIDES
Annual Totals

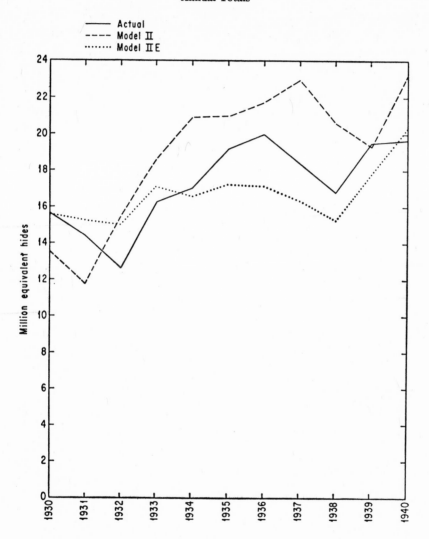

Chart 34

RETAIL SHOE PRICE

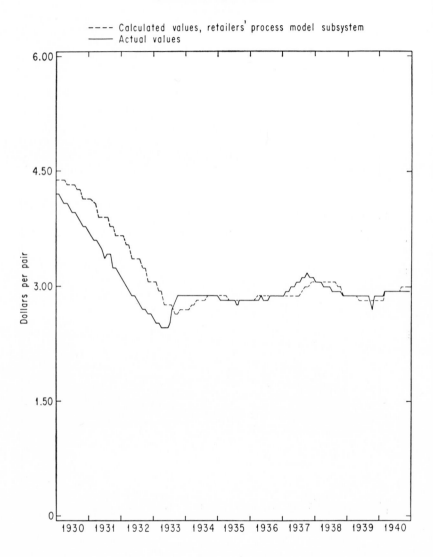

---- Calculated values, retailers' process model subsystem
—— Actual values

Chart 35

RETAILERS' RECEIPTS OF SHOES

---- Calculated values, retailers' process model subsystem
——— Actual values

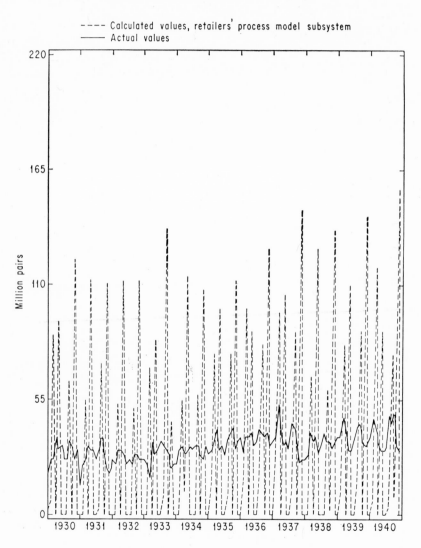

Chart 36

MANUFACTURERS' SHOE PRODUCTION

---- Calculated values, retailers' process model subsystem
—— Actual values

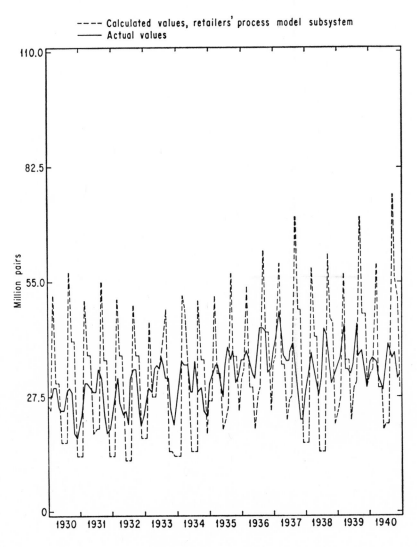

130

Chart 37

MANUFACTURERS' RECEIPTS OF LEATHER

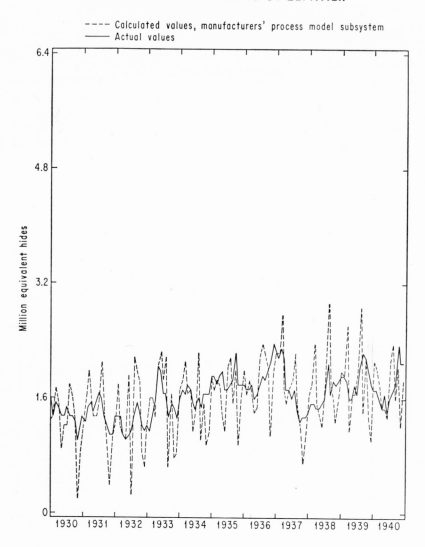

---- Calculated values, manufacturers' process model subsystem
——— Actual values

Chart 38

RETAIL SHOE PRICE

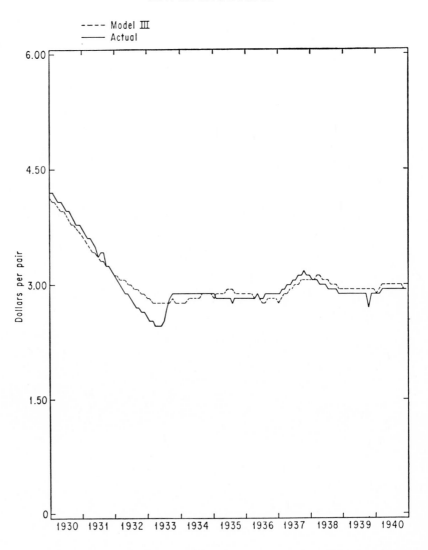

Chart 39

RETAIL SHOE PRICE

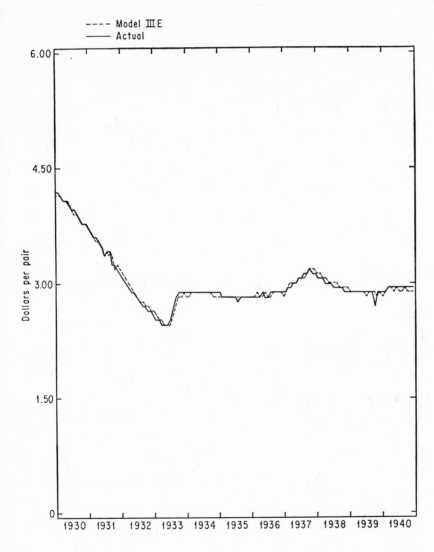

Chart 40

FACTORY SHOE PRICE

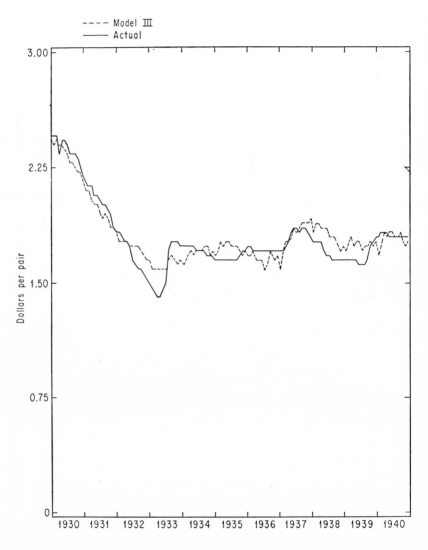

Chart 41

FACTORY SHOE PRICE

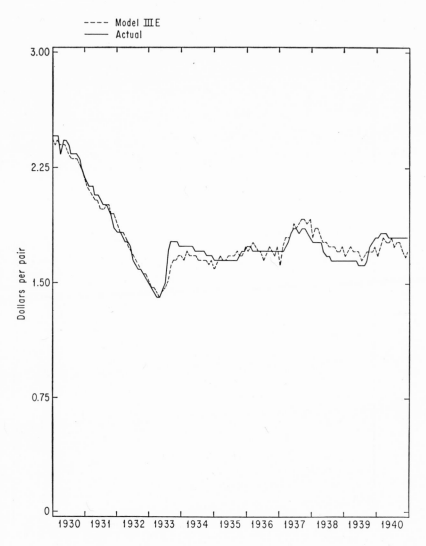

---- Model III E
—— Actual

Chart 42

LEATHER PRICE

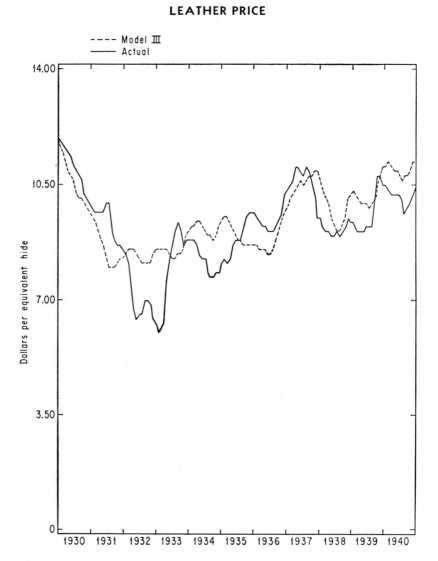

Chart 43

LEATHER PRICE

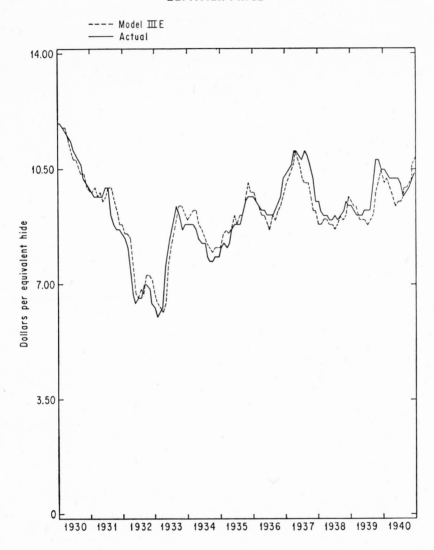

Chart 44

AVERAGE HIDE PRICE

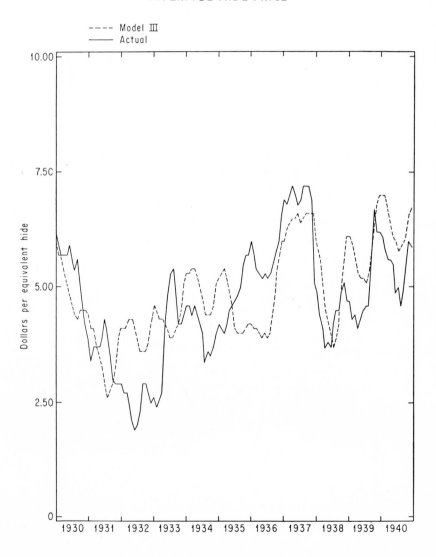

Chart 45

AVERAGE HIDE PRICE

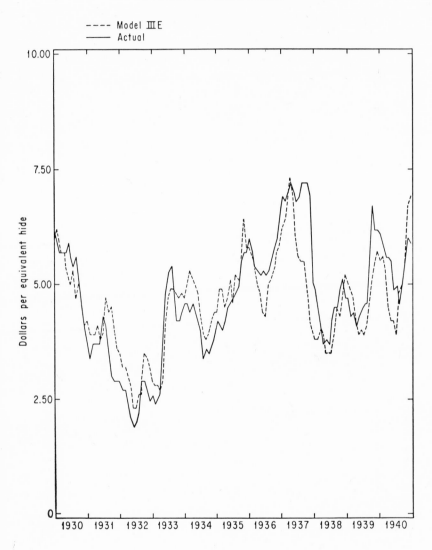

---- Model ⅢE
—— Actual

139

Chart 46

RETAIL SHOE SALES, PAIRS

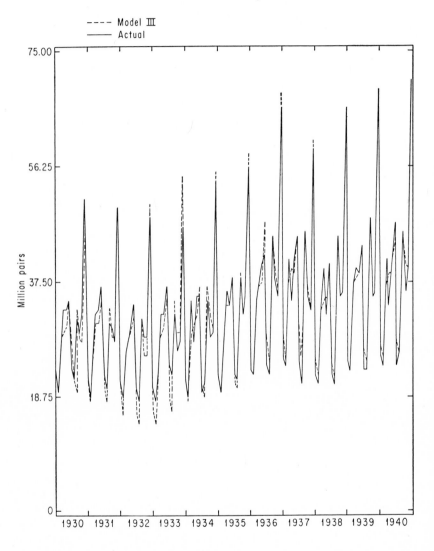

Chart 47

RETAIL SHOE SALES, PAIRS

---- Model III E
——— Actual

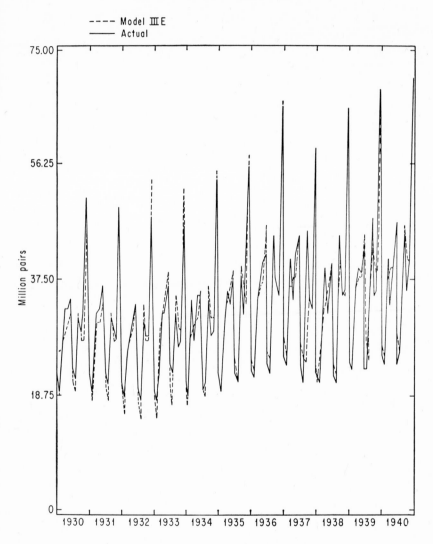

141

Chart 48

RETAILERS' RECEIPTS OF SHOES

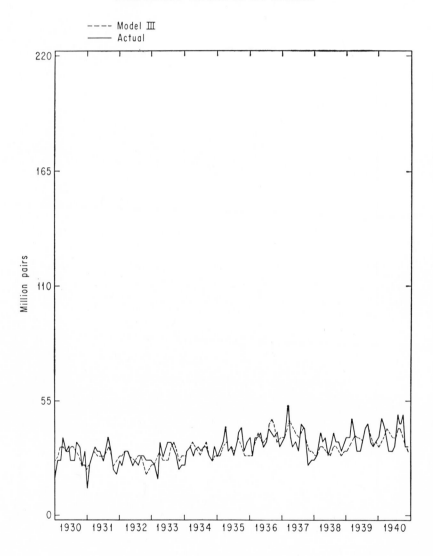

---- Model III
—— Actual

Million pairs

220

165

110

55

0

1930 1931 1932 1933 1934 1935 1936 1937 1938 1939 1940

Chart 49

RETAILERS' RECEIPTS OF SHOES

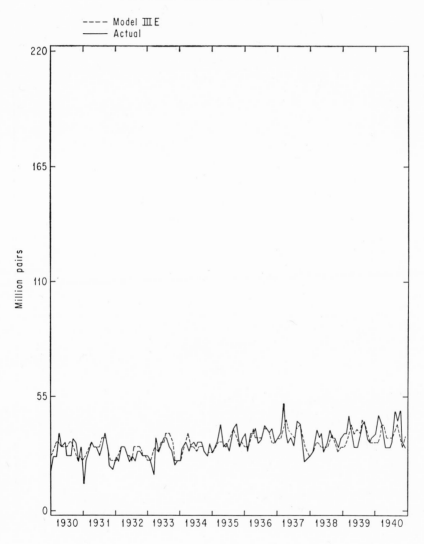

---- Model III E
—— Actual

Million pairs

Chart 50

MANUFACTURERS' SHOE PRODUCTION

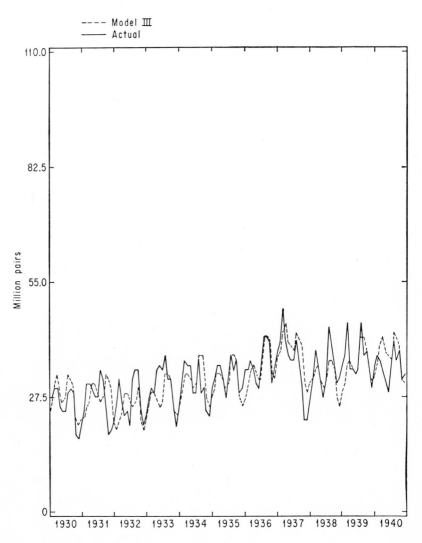

---- Model III
——— Actual

144

Chart 51

MANUFACTURERS' SHOE PRODUCTION

---- Model III E
——— Actual

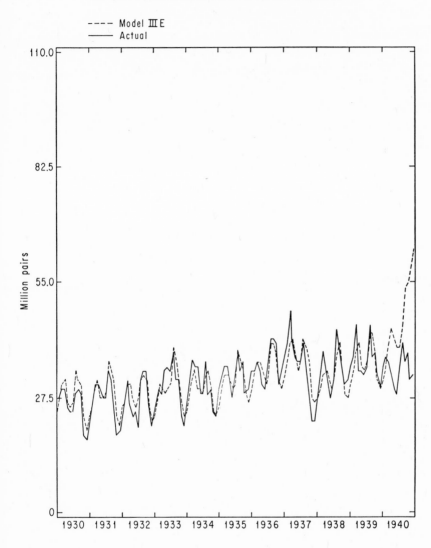

Chart 52

MANUFACTURERS' RECEIPTS OF LEATHER

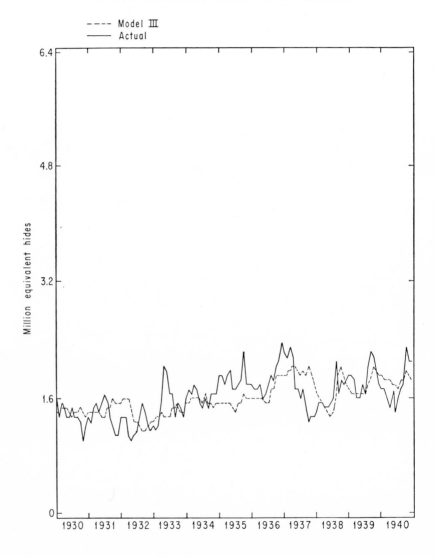

Chart 53

MANUFACTURERS' RECEIPTS OF LEATHER

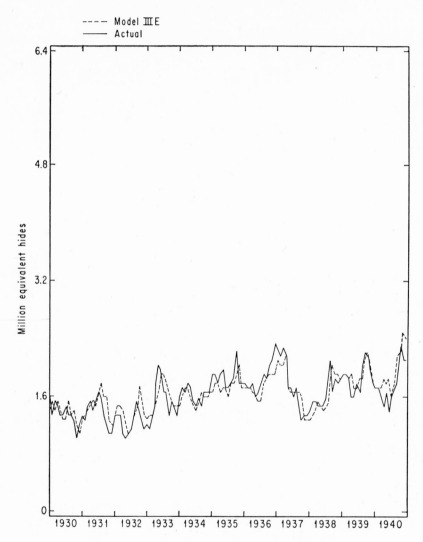

---- Model III E
——— Actual

Chart 54

TANNERS' FINISHED LEATHER PRODUCTION

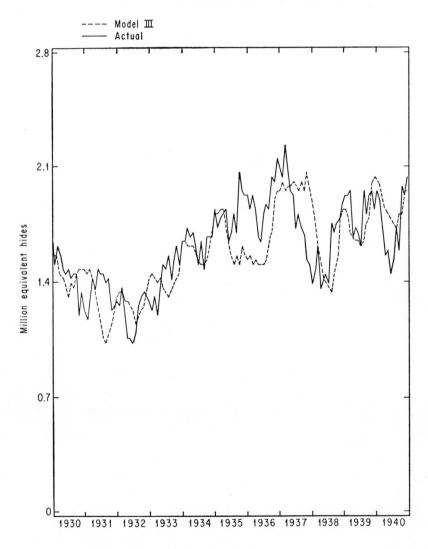

---- Model III
——— Actual

Chart 55

TANNERS' FINISHED LEATHER PRODUCTION

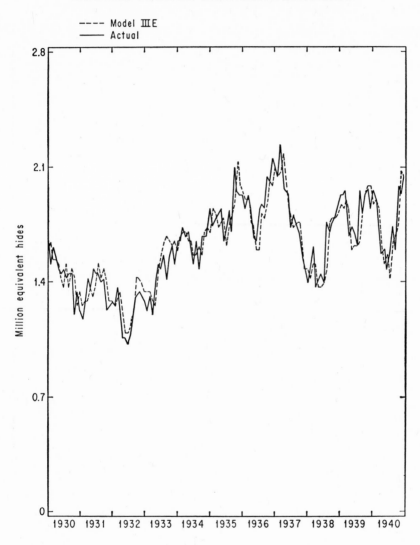

---- Model IIIE
—— Actual

Chart 56

TANNERS' HIDE WETTINGS

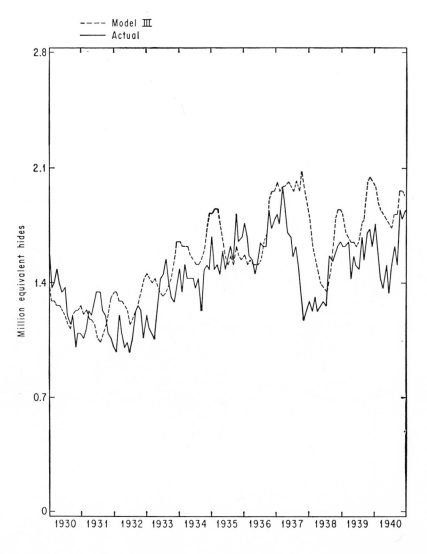

---- Model III
—— Actual

Million equivalent hides

2.8

2.1

1.4

0.7

0

1930 1931 1932 1933 1934 1935 1936 1937 1938 1939 1940

Chart 57

TANNERS' HIDE WETTINGS

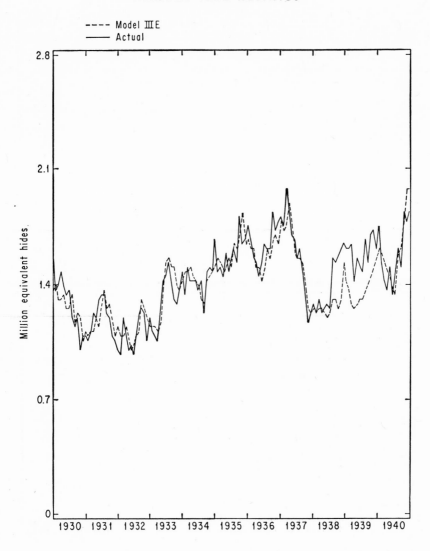

---- Model III E
——— Actual

Million equivalent hides.

2.8
2.1
1.4
0.7
0

1930 1931 1932 1933 1934 1935 1936 1937 1938 1939 1940

Chart 58

TANNERS' RECEIPTS OF ALL HIDES

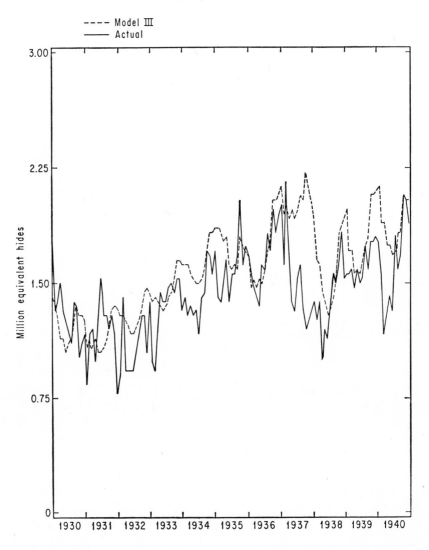

---- Model III
——— Actual

Chart 59

TANNERS' RECEIPTS OF ALL HIDES

---- Model III E
——— Actual

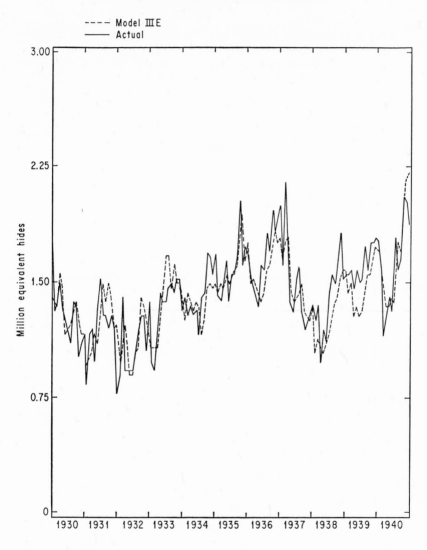

BIBLIOGRAPHY

1. Bach, G. L., *Economics: An Introduction to Analysis and Policy*, 2nd ed., Englewood Cliffs, N. J.: Prentice-Hall, Inc., 1957.

2. Box, G. E. P. and Wilson, K. B., "On the Experimental Attainment of Optimum Conditions," *Journal of the Royal Statistical Society, Series B (Methodological)*, Vol. 13, 1951, pp. 1-45.

3. Charnes, A. and Cooper, W. W., "Management Models and Industrial Applications of Linear Programming," *Management Science*, Vol. 4, No. 1., Oct., 1957, pp. 38-91.

4. Clark, C., "A System of Equations Explaining the United States Trade Cycles, 1921 to 1941," *Econometrica*, Vol. 17, 1949, pp. 93-124.

5. Cyert, R. M., Feigenbaum, E. A., and March, J. G., "Models in a Behavioral Theory of the Firm," *Behavioral Science*, Vol. 4, No. 2, April, 1959, pp. 81-95.

6. Ferber, R., *The Railroad Shippers' Forecasts*, Studies in Business Expectations and Planning, Urbana, Ill.: The University of Illinois, 1953.

7. Forrester, J. W., "Industrial Dynamics — A Major Breakthrough for Decision Makers," *Harvard Business Review*, Vol. 36, No. 4, July–August, 1958, pp. 37-66.

8. Hald, A., *Statistical Theory with Engineering Applications*, New York: John Wiley & Sons, Inc., 1952; London: Chapman & Hall, Ltd., 1952.

9. Henderson, J. M., and Quandt, R. E., *Microeconomic Theory*, New York: McGraw-Hill Book Co., 1958.

10. Hildreth, C. and Jarrett, F. G., *A Statistical Study of Livestock Production and Marketing*, Cowles Commission Monograph No. 15, New York: John Wiley & Sons, Inc., 1955; London: Chapman & Hall, Ltd., 1955.

11. Klein, L. R., *Economic Fluctuations in the United States, 1921–1941*, Cowles Commission for Research in Economics, Monograph No. 11, New York: John Wiley & Sons, Inc., 1950.

12. Klein, L. R., *A Textbook of Econometrics*, Evanston, Illinois: Row, Peterson and Co., 1953.

13. Mack, R. P., *Consumption and Business Fluctuations: A Case Study of the Shoe, Leather, Hide Sequence*, New York: National Bureau of Economic Research, 1956.

14. Mack, R. P., *Factors Influencing Consumption: An Experimental Analysis of Shoe Buying*, Technical Paper 10, New York: National Bureau of Economic Research, 1954.

15. Madansky, A., "The Fitting of Straight Lines When Both Variables Are Subject to Error," *Journal of the American Statistical Association*, Vol. 54, No. 285, March, 1959, pp. 173-205.

16. Modigliani, F., "Business Reasons for Holding Inventories and Their Macro-Economic Implications," *Problems in Capital Formation*, Studies in Income and Wealth, Vol. 19, New York: National Bureau of Economic Research, 1957, pp. 495-506.

17. Perlis, A. J., Smith, J. W., and Van Zoeren, H. R., *Internal Translator (IT), A Compiler for the 650*, 650 Library Program, File Number 2.1.001, Poughkeepsie, New York: IBM Research Center, 1957.

18. Sargan, J. D., "The Estimation of Economic Relationships Using Instrumental Variables," *Econometrica*, Vol. 26, No. 3, July, 1958, pp. 393-415.

19. Theil, H., *Linear Aggregation of Economic Relations*, Amsterdam: North-Holland Publishing Co., 1954.

20. von Szeliski, V. S. and Paradiso, L. J., "Demand for Boots and Shoes as Affected by Price Levels and National Income," *Econometrica*, Vol. 4, 1936, pp. 338-355.

21. Watson, M. A., *Eco omics of Cattlehide Leather Tanning*, Chicago: Rumpf Publishing Co., 1950.